Praise for *Power Entertaining*

"It's not overly dramatic to say your professional destiny can hang on the impression you make. If you are meeting or hosting prospective clients or employers at a reception or business meal, read this book first. Its "I didn't know that" insights and page-turning stories show how to handle yourself with savoir faire so you're the one they relate to, respect, remember, and want to work with."

—Sam Horn
The Intrigue Expert;
Author of *POP!* and *SerenDestiny*

"Finally, we have a book on how to cement business relationships that last. Eddie Osterland shares the rare entertaining insights that can create a memorable experience for those you care about in your life and work. It is not only an art, but a defined strategy for growing your business or organization. This is a must-read for every business owner, executive, and professional in the marketplace!"

—Mark LeBlanc
President of Small Business Success;
Author of *Growing Your Business* and *Never Be the Same*

"Master Sommelier and outstanding Vistage speaker Eddie Osterland notes that most people 'treat wine as a beverage, not as a true partner to good food.' CEOs and executives should understand that if they treat wine as more than a beverage, it can be the perfect complement to cultivating and strengthening their business relationships. Eddie shows us how, as his book expands our knowledge, sensibilities, and opportunities."

—Rafael Pastor
Chairman of the Board and Chief Executive Officer,
Vistage International, Inc.

"Edmund Osterland is not only America's First Master Sommelier, he is a brilliant businessman who understands the principles of how to make occasions special. He can show you how to make any meeting or event a more memorable and impactful event. His mastery is matching the elements to the intended results. He has toured the world training senior executives in the finer touches of leadership and gracious business practices. Let him show you how to make your business dealings more fun and more creative. I learn from him and admire him. You will, too!"

—Jim Cathcart
Past President of the National Speakers Association;
Author of *Relationship Selling*

"Eddie Osterland is one of the most dynamic, entertaining, and knowledgeable wine experts in America."

—Kevin Zraly
Windows on the World Complete Wine Course

"Eddie has a finely honed palate and a special knack for creating exciting wine and food pairings. His enthusiasm when sharing his knowledge about wine and wine tasting is infectious, informative, and very much down to earth. Not only does Eddie know his subject like few others, he knows how to communicate his vast experience and ideas in a fun and easy-to-understand manner."

—Jeffrey Davies
Signature *Jeffrey M. Davies* Selections

POWER
ENTERTAINING

POWER ENTERTAINING

Secrets to Building Lasting Relationships,
Hosting Unforgettable Events, and Closing Big
Deals from America's 1st Master Sommelier

EDDIE OSTERLAND

WILEY

John Wiley & Sons, Inc.

Published by John Wiley & Sons, Inc., Hoboken, New Jersey.
Published simultaneously in Canada.

For general information on our other products and services or for technical support, please contact our Customer Care Department within the United States at (800) 762-2974, outside the United States at (317) 572-3993 or fax (317) 572-4002.

Wiley publishes in a variety of print and electronic formats and by print-on-demand. Some material included with standard print versions of this book may not be included in e-books or in print-on-demand. If this book refers to media such as a CD or DVD that is not included in the version you purchased, you may download this material at http://book support.wiley.com. For more information about Wiley products, visit www.wiley.com.

Library of Congress Cataloging-in-Publication Data:
Osterland, Edmund A.
    Power Entertaining: Secrets to Building Lasting Relationships, Hosting Unforgettable Events, and Closing Big Deals from America's 1st Master Sommelier / Eddie Osterland.
    Includes index.
    ISBN: 978-1-118-26902-2 (cloth)
    ISBN: 978-1-118-28344-8 (ebk)
    ISBN: 978-1-118-28475-9 (ebk)
    ISBN: 978-1-118-28722-4 (ebk)
       1. Business entertaining. 2. Public relations. 3. Strategic alliances (Business).
    4. Success in business. I. Title.
HD59
650.1'3—dc23
                                                                            2012022845

Printed in the United States of America
10 9 8 7 6 5 4 3 2 1

*This book is dedicated to the late Henry J. van der Voort
(1915–2008). Henry was the proprietor of Château
Bellegrave, Pauillac, Bordeaux.
I met Henry late one evening in a Honolulu restaurant, where
I was working as a wine steward. Henry was impressed with my
passion with wine and suggested I study it seriously under the
famed Dr. Emile Peynaud at the Université de Bordeaux. He
graciously offered to set me up in language school in France and
personally introduced me to Dr. Peynaud. The rest is history as I
became the first American Master Sommelier while in Bordeaux,
and I owe it all to Henry, the most elegant, generous, and
good-living gentleman I have ever met.*

Contents

Foreword

The old adage, "It's not what you know, it's who you know," has been a popular business maxim for many years. Unfortunately, this statement misses the mark, and we need to add an element to it that makes it all worthwhile.

> It's not what you know.
> It's not who you know.
> It's *how* you know them, and
> It's how they *feel* about you that matters.

The marketplace has changed dramatically in the past few years, and loyalty seems to be a thing of the past. Forging new connections and establishing and cementing key relationships with prospects, customers, and your advocates can make you successful. Failure to take the strategies and ideas offered in this book can break your success.

Every once in a while you meet someone who has a certain something about him or her. It's the way that person thinks, talks, and interacts with others. You know something is different, but you can't put your finger on it. I believe these special people have a sense of clarity and expertise that cannot be denied. Eddie Osterland is one of those rare people you not only want to know but want to know what he knows.

Eddie has captured the essence of what it means to live life and to create an experience that transcends the norm of entertaining for business or for pleasure. Not only does he provide you with what you need to know, he also provides you with what you need to do to get your groove on and improve your odds in the game of business.

His enthusiasm is infectious, and his commitment to helping others is clearly evident in how he serves others, both personally and professionally. This may be the one book you read this year that can have the most impact on your career.

The best piece of advice I can give you is to devour this book. Keep it within arm's reach and refer to it often. Take action on what you learn, and you will have a greater likelihood of succeeding by design, not by accident.

We're often judged by the company we keep. We're respected for the company that keeps us. Start reading now and you will find out how simple this can be and how fast you can experience the rewards of relationship building. You will discover that a life you can taste is a life worth living and sharing with others.

—Mark LeBlanc
Small Business Success;
Author, *Growing Your Business* and *Never Be the Same*

Preface

Have you taken a colleague to lunch lately? Why not invite him or her out today—
and include a few other people from different parts of your company or business
network. Soon, you'll have an ever-expanding web of friends and contacts.
—Keith Ferrazzi
Author, *Never Eat Alone*

Why I Wrote This Book

You're at a fancy downtown restaurant for dinner with a new
client. A million-dollar business deal is on the table. The waiter
hands you the wine list. Now what?

You wonder, "To make a good impression, should I spend $350 on
the Cabernet Sauvignon 2001 Hillside Select? Or, do I go with something half that price that the client will like *just* as much—maybe more?"

The problem is you don't know what makes a good Cabernet,
much less the Hillside Select. After all, you went to business school,
not bartender's academy!

"What if I order the wrong wine?" you say to yourself. "I'll
embarrass myself and might lose the deal!" For all you know, your
client is a passionate wine collector and connoisseur, with a trove of
1,000 bottles of vintage Bordeaux gathering dust in a wine cellar.

Your forehead begins to break out in a cold sweat. You *have* to
make the right decision.

Who would have thought that your shiny Ivy League MBA,
powerful business connections, and past successes doing big business deals would help so little now? What matters right now, at *this*
moment, is your wine IQ—and your ability to entertain this client
in a way he or she will never forget. In a way that will cement your
relationship with him or her for years to come.

So, what do you do?

That's where I come in. I'm Eddie Osterland (known to my friends as "Eddie O"). I'm a Master Sommelier (MS), and if I may say so, one of America's foremost wine and food coaches! I was the very first American ever to earn this title (of MS), and I can help you make the right choice of wine on this occasion and in countless other business situations as well. For the past 25 years I've been giving advice on business entertaining to CEOs and companies all over the world. I even coined a term, *power entertaining*, to describe what I do. And it's the title of this book!

I love my job. It's actually my passion and my mission in life. Or, as the wine-loving French might say, mon *métier* and *mission*— to educate people about fine wine and food and how to put them together in enjoyable combinations.

In *Power Entertaining* you'll see me display my passion for wine, food, and entertaining as I outline dozens of ways that you can entertain others with flair and confidence, be it at business dinners, client appreciation events, sales meetings, conferences, team retreats, business receptions, retirement functions, or office parties.

Become the Ultimate Business Host!

For example, when it comes to hosting business dinners, banquets, or important client events, I'll show you how to:

- Entertain clients with ease, class, and confidence, using good wine and food as the ingredients to build strong and lasting business relationships.
- Delight colleagues and friends by serving delicious pairings of wine and food that they'll remember for years.
- Transform boring business meetings and sales functions into memorable social events that people will *want* to attend again and again.
- Use business entertaining as a business development and client relations *strategy*.

Impress Clients When You Take Them to Dinner!

But wait; there's more—as all those late-night infomercials always say. I'll also show you how to entertain clients and business associates with style when you take them out on the town or to dinner at a nice restaurant. You'll learn how to:

- Impress clients and colleagues with your intimate knowledge of fine wine and food.
- Order with confidence from restaurant wine lists.
- Select, taste, and appreciate fine wines just as master wine tasters do!
- Close big business deals by ordering just the right wine for the occasion.
- Get the best possible customer service from waiters and the bartenders, even in restaurants known for their world-class attitude.
- Charm (even surprise) business associates into seeing why they must start doing (or keep doing) business with you.

Take Your Home Entertaining to a Whole New Level

And there's still more you'll get from reading *Power Entertaining*. For example, I'll show you how to take your home entertaining to a new level, in ways that will wow your family and friends alike. You'll:

- Learn the basics of casual (but classy) home-based entertaining using wine and food to create unforgettable social events for family and friends.
- Learn about fun and fabulous foodie websites where you can buy exotic items such as tuna belly and acorn-fed ham to serve to friends and family.
- Learn how to find, select, and serve wines from many countries and teach people something about these wines at the same time.

Finally, here's still other stuff you'll learn from reading *Power Entertaining*:

- How to start and stock a home wine cellar
- How to entertain without getting stressed
- How to bond with wine merchants and sommeliers in your local community, people who can help you plan business and home events
- Why your palate is unique to you (as unique as your fingerprints) and why developing a taste for good wine and food involves learning to trust your judgment about what you like

I want you to enjoy this book because I wrote it for you! I want you to learn to love good wine, good food, and entertaining as much as I do. And the power entertaining tips I share in this book are intended to do exactly that. They'll help you entertain others with ease, enjoyment, and self-confidence—in a variety of business and social situations.

This isn't a book about wine per se (there are many other fine books out there on that topic). But this is perhaps the *only* book on the market today that focuses on how to use the *power* of good wine and food to impress your boss, clients, friends, and family.

So, my friend, why not open up a bottle of your favorite white or red wine right now, take a sip, and then take a deep dive into this book. Prepare to enjoy yourself, and may your next business function or client meeting over wine and food be a roaring and enjoyable success—for you and your clients alike!

All the best!

Acknowledgments

As I reflect on my career as a sommelier, and on the writing of this book, I realize that there are many individuals who helped shape me into the person I am today and who continue to guide and enrich my life in wonderful ways. I owe all of them tremendous debts of gratitude.

My parents, Edmund and Nancy Osterland, instilled in me a deep passion and love for entertaining. My mother worked in New York City as a cabaret singer and pianist and performed regularly with jazz legend Bill Evans. My dad, who lived to the ripe old age of 98, was an elegant man and consummate host. Together, the two of them threw the best parties in my neighborhood when I was growing up as a kid in Mountain Lakes, New Jersey, in the late 1950s and early 1960s. I learned a lot from them about how to throw a good party and, more important, how to extend warm hospitality to others. No doubt it's due in part to them that the word *parties* was the one-word descriptor that appeared beneath my high school yearbook picture!

My dear late wife, Vera, with whom I shared so many wonderful moments, was also a major influence on me. She died a few years ago of cancer, but she is forever in my memories. I am forever indebted to her for blessing me with my wonderful daughter, Elissa. Elissa is, in many ways, a chip off the old block and then some. Like her dad, she is a major foodie (maybe even a bigger one than I), and I have so enjoyed the moments we've shared over good food and wine at various spots around the world. You are my pride and joy!

I have many wonderful friends, colleagues, and mentors whom I want to thank for enriching my life and career over the years. They include Dr. Emile Peynaud and Henry van der Voort. These two gentlemen introduced me to the wonderful world of wine and contributed greatly to my formal training and education in Oenology. I also want to acknowledge the other European wine professionals who put their mark on me: Margrit Goebels, George Spanek, Yves de Boisredon, and Jeffrey Davies.

There are others to thank as well.

To Alan Kates, Marcie Rothman, Chris Gluck, Sam Horn, and the ubiquitous Brett Uprichard of Honolulu, who have given me tremendous assistance with writing and marketing support over the years. To my graphic designers, Dave Prescott (www.btwelve.com) and Bob Dunnican (R.W. Dunnican Designs), for their wonderful graphic support; and to Lori Barber and Mike Zemans at SiteLab Interactive (www.sitelab.com), who are responsible for my website and the day-to-day marketing of Eddie Osterland; and to my best friend, SiteLab chief executive officer (CEO) Marlene Matheson.

To my great San Diego buddies—the "Super Somms"—Jesse Rodriguez and Brian Donegan, as well as San Diego wine merchants John Lindsay and Damon Goldstein. Thanks for all the help you provided me as I conducted research for this book. You gave many hours of your time to supporting this project. Thanks also to my dear friend, the brilliant San Diego businessman Lou Ryan.

To the Guild of Sommeliers and its chief operating officer, Geoff Kruth, MS. The Guild exists to further the education and professionalism of all sommeliers and other wine professionals who work in the food, beverage, and hospitality industries. I want to acknowledge the Guild's cooperation and assistance to me as I prepared certain portions of this book. Your help was invaluable.

To the National Restaurant Association (NRA). Many years ago I worked for the NRA and published a book under its auspices. Certain material that appeared in that book has been adapted, updated, and expanded for inclusion in *Power Entertaining*.

To my wonderful assistants over the years: Theresa O'Neil, Janet Hatch, Diane Roberts Vassos, and Susie Conklin.

To my amazing instrument flight instructor, Robert D. Greene, the coolest 86-year-old dude on this planet. I learned so much about flying (and life) from you!

To the wine guys and gal with whom I was lucky enough to spend five years in New York City: Rory Callahan, Kevin Zraly, Joshua Wesson, Alex Joerger, Mary Mulligan, Daniel Johnnes, Michael Madrigale, Joey de Lissio, Michael Skurnik, Steve Olsen, and Steve Fox. Anyone who knows you, knows what a pleasure it is to work with you and be your friend.

To the best literary agent in the world, Doris Michaels (www .dsmagency.com) and her former associate, Delia Berrigan Fakis. Thanks to both of you for believing in this project!

To some of the amazing Master Sommeliers I've had the pleasure to know over the years and who have taught me so much about our profession: Nunzio Alioto, Andrea Immer Robinson, David Glancy, Evan Goldstein, Tim Gaiser, Emmanuel Kemiji, Guy Stout, Larry O'Brien, Madeleine Triffon, Richard Dean, Luis de Santos, Fred Dexheimer, Greg Harrington, Jay Fletcher, Robert Bath, Laura De Pasquale, Wayne Belding, and the infamous Fred Dame.

Last, I want to thank my great friend and collaborator Richard Koonce (www.richardkoonce.com), without whom this book would not have been possible.

Introduction

I Love This Job!

How does a guy like me, a kid from New Jersey, grow up to become America's first Master Sommelier? To tell you that, I have to take you back to the tender days of my youth.

After graduating from college in 1968 with a degree in psychology, I decided to go to Hawaii with a buddy of mine for the summer. During my first two weeks in Honolulu, I soaked in the rays, ogled the babes, and fell in love with at least five different women. But then my mother called.

"Eddie, when are you coming home?"

I'd already decided *never!* But how do you say that to your *mother?* So I told her, "Mom, you won't believe this, but I got into grad school here at the University of Hawaii and just landed a great job in one of Waikiki's finest restaurants. I've even bought a car and rented an apartment!" I told her I didn't need money (music to any parent's ears) but that I had to go because I was "so friggin' busy."

Now, truth be told, everything I told her was a lie. But I figured I could make it all come true soon enough.

I did, in fact, enroll at the University of Hawaii, and then shopped around for a nighttime job to support my schooling. And since I knew what a shrimp cocktail was, I applied for a waiter's position at The Ilikai, one of Hawaii's finest hotels. I told a nice lady in the hotel's human resources (HR) department about my *vast* work experience in restaurants, and guess what? They hired me! Okay, maybe I lied a little here, too, but my fantasy got me into their best restaurant, The Top of the I.

Once on the job, I learned quickly. Nobody seemed to notice my ineptitude, and I quickly earned enough money to share an apartment in Manoa Valley with my buddy and buy myself a Volkswagen Beetle. Back in those days, a bug was the "in" car because you could drive around with your surfboard sticking up through the sunroof. I didn't surf, but God it was a great chick magnet. Life was good!

One evening at work, while polishing glassware before the dinner service, I saw Anton, the maître d', cruising around the dining room. In his hand was a silver chain with a big cellar key and tasting cup attached to it. It was what the French sommelier, Pierre, wore every night.

Suddenly Anton stopped in front of me, hung the chain around my neck, and said, "Pierre just called in sick, and I need you to sub for him tonight."

I knew nothing about wine, so I said, "No way! I can't do that."

Anton leered at me, said he had enough problems on his hands that night without having to deal with me, and then read me the riot act.

"You want to keep your job here right? Well, listen up, white wine goes with fish. Red wine goes with meat. If anybody's on the fence, pitch 'em a rosé like Lancer's or Mateus. That's all you need to know!"

Not having a choice, I picked up the wine list. I opened it in the middle and the first wine on the page was #131, Château Timberlay, a Bordeaux.

"Nice and fruity with a crisp, clean finish, $16.00," it said. Sounded good to me!

Before I could study the full list, a customer at table 6 asked for the wine steward. Reluctantly, I approached his table.

"My wife is having scampi, and I am having the rack of lamb, medium-rare," he said. "What wine would you suggest?"

I was really nervous. "I suggest #131, Château Timberlay. It is a *Bor-Ducks*" (my feeble attempt at pronouncing *Bordeaux*). "Nice and fruity with a crisp, clean finish, and it goes well with meat," I stammered.

"Well, if you recommend it, we'll give it a try!" he said.

I brought the bottle to the table, opened it, and, shaking, poured both of them a glass. He tasted it; then she tasted it. She smiled at him, he smiled at me, and then he gave me $3.00. "That's an excellent choice!" he said.

"But, of course!" I said, pointing to myself. "I am *the* sommelier!"

A moment later, another man raised his hand from across the dining room. He said, "The wife and I are from Oklahoma, and we're gonna have that cattleman's cut, the 2.2-pound porterhouse, *well-done*. What'dya recommend with that?"

Without missing a beat I said, "Why, the #131 Château Timberlay at $16.00. It's a *Bor-Ducks*. Nice 'n fruity with a crisp, clean finish. It goes great with a well-done porterhouse steak!" I was on a roll.

"Young man, if that's what you recommend we'll have a bottle!" he said exuberantly. So, I poured each of them a glass. She tasted it first, smiled at her husband, and said, "This is wonderful." With that, the guy gave me a couple of bucks tip. I was beginning to like this job!

At the end of the night all the waiters sat down at a table, and as we cooled our heels, we also counted our tips. It turned out that I'd made twice as much in tips serving wine that night as I had serving food. And, of course, I didn't know diddly-squat about wine!

I said to myself, "I love this job!"

After that night, I served wine on Pierre's days off and waited tables the rest of the week. One day I heard there was an opening for a full-time wine steward down the road at an Italian restaurant, The Trattoria. I applied and got the job. I didn't know a thing about Italian wine but figured I could learn on the job.

As the restaurant's *vinaio* (Italian for sommelier), one of my responsibilities was to restock the wines on the wine list. This gave me the opportunity to meet many wine salespeople and taste their wines. Thanks to them, my knowledge of wine grew. One of the people I met was a guy named George Spanek, General Manager of Bercut-Vandervoort, a San Francisco–based wine importer. George lived in the continental United States, but his territory included Honolulu. Although The Trattoria was an Italian restaurant, he insisted that I put one of his French wines, Château Bellegrave from Bordeaux, on my *Italian* wine list. Why? He said he needed to place the wine on as many wine lists as he could because the CEO of his company, Henry J. van der Voort was the owner of Château Bellegrave.

I thought, "What the hell? We ought to have at least one French wine on the list. To round out our wine cellar."

One evening, George told me that his boss was coming to Honolulu the following month and that he'd suggested he dine at my restaurant. He told me I should be excited. "You will meet one of America's most highly regarded wine personalities," he said with a smile.

The evening came that Monsieur van der Voort was booked at our restaurant for dinner. That day was a hectic and tiring one for me at school, but I arrived at the restaurant full of youthful adrenaline. I was psyched to impress this guy when he arrived, so I hatched myself a plan.

That night, whenever customers asked for wine recommendations, instead of suggesting the usual Valpolicella, Chianti, or Barbaresco (as I typically did), I recommended just one thing: the 1966 Château Bellegrave. In a few cases people hesitated at first, but when I told them the restaurant's chef, "Luigi" used the Château Bellegrave in the sauce that accompanied their entrées, most of them readily acquiesced. And in cases where this didn't work, my last tactic (which always sealed the deal) was to pour them a sample of the wine. It turns out nobody can resist a free sample of vino that the sommelier sends to their table!

By the time 8 o'clock rolled around, I had placed 19 bottles of Château Bellegrave on tables surrounding the table reserved for Monsieur van der Voort. I'd choreographed things perfectly!

At the stroke of eight, Monsieur van der Voort and his entourage arrived at the restaurant. When he noticed that people at nearly every table were drinking a bottle of his 1966 Château Bellegrave at an Italian restaurant, he said to his waiter, Jean Jacques, "*Eh bien mon vieux, qu'est ce qui se passe ici?*" ("What's going on here?")

He wanted to know who was responsible for this. With that, the waiter pointed at me and said, "That guy over there." Monsieur van der Voort motioned me to his table and asked me why I'd done this. I told him I was trying to make a good impression on him. He said I had, and asked me to join him after I got off work.

Later that night we had a long talk, and he told me that he felt my passion for wine far surpassed any interest I had in behavioral psychology. He also said that if I really wanted to pursue my wine studies, I should do it at the famous Institut d'Oenologie at the

Université de Bordeaux, France. He added that if I were interested, he'd make the necessary introductions to get me in.

I was ecstatic—until he said I must be fluent in French! But he allayed my fears by saying I could take care of that with an additional year of study at the Université de Poitiers, and then offered to arrange an introduction for that as well.

Then he told me to call him *Henry*.

I told Henry I would think about his kind offer. So, over the next day or so, I thought about what it would mean to leave beautiful Honolulu; my wonderful girlfriend, Lani; and all my friends. It would be tough, but then again, I had a passion for wine that had been with me for years. Not only did I like to drink it, but I loved to serve it and entertain with it as well. I was a *joie de vivre* kind of guy who loved organizing parties for my friends and hosting them with both good wine and good food. Now, Henry was giving me a chance to formally pursue a career in a field I really loved. I knew this was my calling and was what I wanted to do with the rest of my life. My apprehension lasted about a day. Then I called Henry.

I didn't have enough money to pursue my new studies, so I had to work another nine months to save enough cash for wine school. Then I moved to France to study the language, and before long, I enrolled in the university and earned the prestigious degree, diplôme d'aptitude à la dégustation des vins, or DUAD, after three years of study.

But things didn't end there. In Europe, the highest distinction for a sommelier is that of Master Sommelier, a title bestowed only on completion of a rigorous and harrowing wine exam. I wondered if I could be that good and decided to give it a shot. I studied and studied and studied and took the exam, passing all three sections on my first try. With that I became America's first Master Sommelier in 1973—at the tender age of 28!

So that's how I got my start in the wine business—through the generosity of a wonderful friend and benefactor, Henry, who saw my passion for wine and was willing to help me turn my interest in wine into a career. But the story of my journeyman days as a sommelier doesn't end there. In fact, there's a funny footnote to this story that makes me both chuckle *and* wince to this day.

After passing the Master Sommelier exam, it was time for me to return to America. Four years in France had been nice, but it had also taught me to appreciate things like big cars, Big Macs, free enterprise, and the kind of chicks I'd met in Hawaii. Nothing against France—I now spoke the language with aplomb. But I really was hankering for home.

As it turned out, though, getting back home wouldn't be that easy and would wind up costing me a king's ransom in wine—all because of the car I owned!

While studying in France I had bought a beat-up Fiat 600 from a friend for $150. It was already about 20 years old when I bought it, but at least it ran. In fact, I drove that car for three years while in wine school in Bordeaux. For the first two years, the car worked fine. I drove it everywhere, exploring the French countryside on week-ends, visiting châteaux, sampling great wines, and collecting bottles of fine vintages that I tucked away in the car's trunk and hauled back with me to my student apartment.

Then one day I hit a bump in the road—in France these things are often the size of sink holes—and lost the car's starter motor. Too expensive to replace, I wound up driving the car for the next two years without a starter motor, jump-starting it when I needed to by pushing it or parking on a hill, releasing the brake, and letting the car roll gently downhill when I needed to get it going in the morning for class. I did this for *two* years!

At times operating this Mixmaster of a car with its 26-horsepower toy engine was really comical. A tiny thing (by American standards) when you started it, it sounded more like a very large household appliance than a motor vehicle. But it was fun to drive and generally reliable, and parking it was never a problem! In fact, I found this really neat parking space at the top of a hill near where I lived as a student in Bordeaux that was always available because nobody else would park there. (Yeah, you guessed it; it was right next to a fire hydrant.) For two years I collected unpaid parking tickets on the car, considering it the price I had to pay to drive a car with no starter motor.

But now, as I prepared to leave Bordeaux for the last time, I was concerned. The car was as rickety as a rickshaw, mostly because of all the miles I'd put on it over the years. Even after losing the starter motor, I'd continued my weekend jaunts to the countryside to sample and buy wine. What's more, I had continued to collect parking tickets that the *gendarmes* had placed on my car's windshield several times a week. By this time, I had more than 100 of them tucked away in the glove box. All unpaid!

Still, I thought the car had enough life in it for one last road trip from Bordeaux to Paris for my flight home. But little did I know . . .

As I packed my stuff for the flight to the States, my most treasured possessions were 116 unopened bottles of some of the finest wine in the world, bottles that I'd collected during four years of weekend wine romps through the French countryside. I had collected a wine cellar's worth of vintages that was worth thousands in today's dollars.

I couldn't take all these bottles with me on the plane, of course, so, I shipped 100 bottles to the United States ahead of me. Thank God! The remaining 16 bottles—some of the best in the lot—would travel with me from Bordeaux to New York.

On the day of my departure from Bordeaux, I left the city around noon with an open bottle of 10-franc wine to drink on the way. It was an 11-hour drive to Paris, and for the first few hours, I drove merrily along, breathing in the French country air, mulling my future, and serenely sipping wine as the ancient French countryside passed quietly behind me

And then trouble!

About 9 hours into the trip, just 2 hours short of Paris, a light flickered on the car's dashboard. I wanted to ignore it, but I knew what it meant. The light flickered amber for a few moments and then turned to a solid red.

Uh ohhh . . .

I pulled the car over and tried to figure out what to do. Although I had my ticket with me for my return flight, I didn't have so much as a franc in my pocket in the event of a roadside emergency or accident. (Remember, I was a student!)

I didn't know what to do. I couldn't turn the engine off because I knew I'd never get it started again. (At this point the car was too heavy to push because it was so full of my stuff!) There was no way I could knock on anybody's door to ask for help because it was late at night, and if somebody called the police, they'd find 100 unpaid parking tickets in my glove box and I'd be dragged off to a French jail never to be heard from again.

Making matters worse, I had never insured the car during my years in France (a requirement of French law), so I was afraid of having my passport confiscated and my wine impounded and getting hauled before an unsympathetic French magistrate for God knows what kind of punishment.

Yes, I was in deep shit. Or *merde*, as the French say.

So I went to the back of the car and flipped open the hood to stare at the engine. After all, that's what *real* men do right?

Then I got it. The engine was overheating. I thought for a moment and came up with the perfect solution. I unzipped my fly and took aim at my car's now clattering engine. The only problem was it was dark and I didn't notice the spinning radiator fan. The result, shall we say, was like "spitting in the wind"; everything came right back to me, soaking my pants without giving any relief to the exasperated engine! Ugh. Now what?

Then it hit me. I had lots of wine on board. Oh God, had it come to this?

I went back to the front of the car, opened the first box of wine and took out a bottle. It was a 1959 Château Mouton Rothschild. I pulled out the cork, took a sip, said, "Oh my God!," and poured it into the car's dry radiator. I still remember the sound it made, *Glug, glug-glug-glug, glug, glug-glug, glug* . . .

I watched the dashboard hopefully, but the red dashlight stayed on. Damn!

I pulled out the next bottle, a 1959 Lafite Rothschild. I took a swig, uttered a stronger profanity, and then poured *it* into the radiator. Again, *glug-glug-glug, glug, glug-glug, glug* . . .

No change.

The next vintage I had with me was my 1955. I poured bottles of Château Lafite Rothschild, Château Mouton Rothschild, Château Latour, Château Margaux, and Château Haut Brion (a total of five bottles in all) down into the void, never to be cherished or loved by anyone!

Still the light stayed on.

What the hell? My face was now wet with tears and red with anger. I felt really sorry for myself and angry with myself at the same time!

Then I went to the 1953 vintage. Same volunteers this time—bottles of Lafite, Latour Mouton, Margaux, and Haut Brion. Oy vey! The light didn't flicker, not even for a moment.

Next into the radiator went two bottles of 1961 Hospice de Beaune, Corton, Cuvée Docteur Peste (liquid silk) . . .

Finally, the light went out!

By this time, only one bottle of wine remained. With things finally under control, I got in the car, drove to Paris, left the car running near the airport tarmac, got out with my bottle and little suitcase, and sprinted to board my plane.

Okay, so maybe you're a little skeptical about the veracity of this story. Over the years some people have questioned whether I've exaggerated events here for dramatic effect. One man called me a liar. He was a lawyer. But here are the plain facts. Everything I've said about this story is true. There's no exaggeration. Honest!

You must realize that in 1973, wines we consider priceless today, like the Château Mouton Rothschild, cost only about $10.00 a bottle in Bordeaux. Today, wines like this can go for $500 to $1,000 a bottle!

Now back to the story . . .

The plane took off for America. I sat back in my chair, stinking of wine (and worse), reached into my bag, and pulled out a bottle of 1945 Château Latour (the year I was born).

The girl sitting next to me noticed the label, smiled, said her name was Cheryl, and appeared to ignore my heavy beard, pungent aroma, and disheveled appearance. I pulled the cork and with two hands lifted the bottle to my lips and started drinking.

I was a happy man. After all, I'd achieved my goals. I'd pursued my passion to become a wine expert and become America's first Master Sommelier—and I wasn't even 30.

I'd also learned a classy romance language in the process, steeped myself in European culture, dated a few fabulous French women, and proved how resilient I could be when faced with an overheated Fiat on the edge of a major radiator breakdown.

Life, I decided, was good, and I set myself about the task of achieving my next goal: to bring the joys of good wine, bonhomie, and good food to others. And that's a goal I've achieved with the writing of this book.

So read on, my friend. And above all else: *Amusez-vous bien*. Or as we say in American, enjoy!

1

My Definition of Power Entertaining

More business decisions occur over lunch and dinner than at any other time, yet no MBA courses are given on the subject.

—Peter Drucker

Does the thought of taking a big client to lunch make your palms sweat or cause your stomach to knot up?

Does the idea of hosting a group of business colleagues or major customers at dinner in a fancy restaurant make your heart pound or leave you gasping frantically for breath? I'm serious!

It may be because you think you're bad at small talk, are impatient with "social niceties," or don't know how to properly read a French menu or wine list. (Your mother never taught you this stuff.) Or, maybe it's because you know it was only a year ago that you finally learned the difference between tabbouleh and baba ghanoush—this after stumbling upon the Food Channel one night while channel surfing for another episode of *Law and Order: SVU*.

Or maybe it's because you fear your client (the man or woman you're taking to dinner) knows more about good wine and food than you do, and you don't want to look like some yahoo when he or she orders the halibut cheeks with tempura crosnes (aka Chinese artichoke) and you opt for the 16-ounce sirloin with a side of twice-baked potatoes.

Relax my friend; you're not alone!

Just as many people fear public speaking more than their own death, a lot of us also have a morbid fear of entertaining other people—especially in business settings. Oh yeah, you might be comfortable taking that client buddy of yours for a beer once in a while at that bar down the street from your office. (You know, the place with the loud music where the beers come with nachos and a quart bucket of fried calamari.) But that's as far as you ever go with "business entertaining."

Until now, it hasn't mattered much, either. You've had jobs where business entertaining wasn't really necessary. Or, if it was, it was always a low-key and occasional thing, like taking your secretary to lunch on their birthday, celebrating a colleague's promotion, or buying that occasional lunch for your client buddy you know well.

Now Business Entertaining Is Part of Your Job Description!

But now you're in the big time. Now your job requires you to do business entertaining on a regular basis. You may be:

- A salesperson who must regularly wine and dine clients in nice restaurants
- An executive who often closes big business deals over dinner or cocktails
- A chief executive officer CEO who must play host to business prospects at swanky cocktail receptions, glitzy dinners, and other business social functions
- A corporate banquet or meetings planner who's looking for new ideas in planning office parties, client events, awards dinners, and other business functions
- A banker, lawyer, ad executive, or investment advisor whose clients like to do business over dinner and drinks

- One of the millions of other men and women in business today for whom business entertaining is part of doing the job

Yes, for many people today, business entertaining is part of the job description—at least the *implicit* job description. And now you've realized it's part of your job description, too!

You picked up this book because you realize that you need to develop the skills, know-how, and panache to entertain others with style, ease, and confidence in business situations. In essence, you've decided that you need to master the skills of power entertaining!

What exactly *is* power entertaining, you ask?

As its core, I define power entertaining as the art of building strong business relationships with colleagues and customers, using great wine, food, and hospitality as the currency for bringing people together, creating enjoyable events, fostering interpersonal chemistry, and instilling in people a desire to do business with you and your company or organization.

This book is about giving you the tools and social savoir faire to power entertain with confidence, because doing so can make you a star in your business, somebody whom others will be attracted to and want to do business with time and time again.

Building Business Relationships Is More Important Than Ever!

Building relationships has always been key to success in business, but today it's more important than ever. Business is hypercompetitive, and building and sustaining strong client relationships is critical not just to getting business but to keeping it. Remember the sales adage, "Keeping an existing customer costs a lot less than acquiring a new one"? That's always good advice, but today (given the cost of doing business), it's truer than ever!

Mastering the art of power entertaining will help you both *attract* and *retain* customers. And guess what? It doesn't have to cost you an arm and a leg. You can entertain others with class and style but also at a very reasonable cost. So, I encourage you to make power entertaining a part of your company's business development efforts and marketing mix from this point forward.

There's also a second reason to make power entertaining part of your approach to business development today: by applying power entertaining principles to your interactions with clients, you and your company can get a critical leg up in today's increasingly global business environment. That's right. In today's world we all know that business is increasingly global and cross-cultural in nature. To be successful in this new business world, executives must be able to entertain effectively across multiple countries, cultures, and time zones. Sophistication and worldliness are important, and knowing the subtleties of how to entertain others in a wide variety of situations can make the critical difference when it comes to landing large international clients, closing deals with foreign partners, building relationships with global customers and suppliers, and much, much more.

See where I'm going here?

Let's face it; business entertaining is something you need to know how to do—with skill, charm, knowledge, and self-assuredness.

Thus, the time for you to get over any ambivalence you may have about business entertaining is *now*, my friend. And learning the principles of power entertaining can help you do that. Embracing power entertaining principles and practices will help you start or grow your business. They can help you nurture both new and existing business relationships. They can help you advance in your career and excel in your interactions with others. Bottom line: power entertaining is a unique form of marketing and business development that you can use for a variety of business purposes.

An Entertainment Coach to CEOs

Over the years, I've helped hundreds of business executives and CEOs become successful power entertainers, and my goal in this book is to help you become one, too. What does it take? Just a slight change of mind-set on your part and a willingness to embrace and apply the principles of power entertaining that I outline in these pages. If you conscientiously apply the ideas and suggestions I outline in this book, you, too, can be a power entertainer in whatever realm of life and business you operate!

How Power Entertaining Is Different from Traditional Business Entertaining

For years, many companies have built their business entertaining (and business development efforts) around a simple model of "boozing and schmoozing" clients. Typically this entails businesspeople using their expense accounts to wine and dine clients and business prospects in expensive restaurants or other exclusive venues. And sometimes it involves a company sponsoring big cocktail receptions or sporting events or hosting big business banquets. The premise in all these cases is to throw expensive food and alcohol (sometimes a lot of it) at people with the hope that it will increase sales and improve business relationships. But truth be told, it's often hard to gauge the success and cost-effectiveness of this kind of business entertaining, especially after hotels and caterers are paid and everybody's expense reports have been submitted! And, it's often an excuse for everybody (salespeople and customers alike) to get so heavily hammered while "discussing business" that they don't always *close* the business.

So, is there a better way to do business entertaining? You bet!

Power entertaining differs from traditional business entertaining in at least five ways:

1. *Power entertaining isn't just an excuse to booze and schmooze with clients; it's actually a business development strategy.* It's about creating highly pleasurable social events for people built around great wine, great food, great company, and great ambience. It's also about giving people enjoyable memories of an evening with you (and your company) that will "brand" you in their minds, cause them to remember you fondly, and make them want to do business with you in the future!

2. *Traditional business entertaining often involves large social events featuring lousy hotel food and boring everyday wines of no distinction. In contrast, power entertaining events are often held on a small, intimate scale, featuring sampler menus of delicious foods alongside many different kinds of wine served throughout an evening.* The idea at a power entertaining event is to introduce people to

wines and foods they've never had before and to use this as the catalyst to get people talking and interacting with one another—and with you! The wine is often the star of the show at these events, while the food items served with the wine play an important and savory supporting role.

3. *Traditional business entertaining often includes boring after-dinner speakers that nobody remembers. In contrast, power entertaining events include strong educational and entertainment components, so people leave the event feeling they've learned something (and enjoyed something) that they will long remember.* To inject entertainment and educational components into a power entertaining event, you might decide to:

   a. Have a professional sommelier give a short lecture to people about the finer points of wine tasting.

   b. Introduce people to a selection of wines and appetizers they've never tasted before.

   c. Serve people unusual pairings of wine (for example, comparing American wines and their European counterparts).

   d. Organize wine and food pairings around other specific themes.

   e. Give people who attend your event small gifts and mementos like menus, recipes for the food served, and info about the various wines they sampled that night. All this to create an event that they will long remember.

4. *Power entertaining events give people a better chance to network than occurs at more traditional client events.* At power entertaining functions, guests get to mingle with one another while enjoying the various wine/food pairings you serve to them throughout an evening. This breaks down social barriers, encourages relationship building and interaction, and creates a pleasant shared experience for everybody present.

   Finally, the beauty of my event-proven power entertaining principles is that you can use them to plan and manage events of virtually any size! Yes, you can use them to plan and manage events for hundreds of people in a hotel ballroom (if you really want to). Or, use them to plan an event for just a couple of dozen people at an exclusive restaurant, resort, or country club. You can design an evening to feature a beautifully choreographed series of wine and food pairings served to people over several hours (complete with color commentary on what people are tasting). Or, you can put together just a couple of wine/food combinations to serve people over an hour or two. You can even use power entertaining principles to design intimate one-on-one dinners with your most important clients in five-star hotels, business clubs, or other exclusive settings.

Give People an Unforgettable Experience!

The bottom line here is that power entertaining is all about creating an experience for people, the likes of which they don't normally see—and probably never have experienced—in a business setting before. I like to say that a power entertaining event can be the culinary equivalent of going to see a performance of Cirque du Soleil. Done right, your guests will be blown away, not only by the wine and food you serve, but also by the surprises and delights you tuck into your afternoon or evening event with them.

If you build your next business event around the concepts I've just mentioned, not only will you wow people with your ability to throw a good a party but you'll also give them a great wine and culinary experience that they'll long remember—and always associate with you!

That's a brief overview of what power entertaining as a concept is all about. Think of it as a new operating system to govern how you do client development and business entertaining in the future. I guarantee it works, and this book will show you how.

Chapter Overviews

Following are more details on what you'll find in each chapter of *Power Entertaining*:

- *Chapter 2: Toss (and I Do Mean TOSS) That Caesar Salad!* Want to know how *not* to put on a big business event for a lot of people in a hotel? In this chapter, I tell the story of how I helped save one of my clients from social disaster by helping him plan a menu for a big event that won him kudos with customers and colleagues alike. (I think you'll like the menu I recommended he serve. It's one you could serve, too!)

- *Chapter 3: 20 Secrets of Successful Power Entertaining.* Want to be known as somebody who puts on mind-blowing wine tastings and hospitality events for your clients and colleagues? Chapter 3 lays out 20 power entertaining tips to make you a master of upscale business entertaining in a wide variety of settings. I talk about how to power entertain with style and panache; how to create a total experience for your guests using principles of hospitality, graciousness, and stagecraft; and how to delight your guests with fine wine and good food, great ambience, and careful planning. In writing this chapter, I drew heavily on my many years of experience living, studying, and working in Europe, especially France, where I spent thousands of hours entertaining and serving people as a sommelier in restaurants, at workplaces, and at home.

- *Chapter 4: Power Pairing Great Foods with Great Wines.* Good food and good wine can bring people together at a party like few other things can. To quote my friend and colleague Sam Horn, they are the "international currency for connection" and can set the mood for people to engage, hook up, hang out, and generate "fireworks" with one another. But what about hooking up the right wine with the right food to create *culinary* fireworks at a party or client event? How do you do that? In this chapter, I talk about how to create dramatic and even provocative pairings of wine and food that will make your palate pop and your jaw drop. I describe powerful, even orgasmic combinations of wine and food that are mouthwateringly delicious and unforgettable!

- *Chapter 5: Your New Best Friends: The Sommelier and the Wine Merchant.* In this chapter I emphasize that as a power entertainer, you don't need to become a wine and food expert to act like one. You simply have to have friends in the right places. And that means developing personal relationships with sommeliers and wine merchants in your community and at your favorite restaurants. Taking the initiative to meet such wine professionals can help shape the power entertaining you do and make any event you host a blowout success!

- *Chapter 6: So Many Wines, So Little Time!* In this chapter I first take you on a brief tour of the world of wines and then share more than two dozen suggested wine pairings that you can incorporate into power entertaining events. You'll learn such things as how to distinguish a Beaujolais from a Bordeaux and a Petit Chablis from a Premier Cru, as well as the meaning of words like *terroir* and *flabby*. You'll also learn all the basics for designing power pairings of wines to both delight and impress your guests and keep them talking about your event for days, if not weeks, afterward!

- *Chapter 7: Taste Wine like the Masters Do.* In this chapter I explain how to taste wine as the Masters do and how to enjoy wine tasting to its fullest by using your eyes, nose, and taste buds to assess its quality, complexity, and character. I discuss the tasting methods I learned while a student at the Université de Bordeaux and how you can conduct fun wine tastings with your guests, in part by introducing them to tasting criteria inspired by European wine masters. I conclude the chapter by explaining that although there are many objective criteria for judging a wine, everybody's palate is different—as unique, in fact, as their fingerprints. So, you should discover what *your* palate enjoys, not simply subscribe to what others (including wine critics) say you should enjoy.

- *Chapter 8: Out of the Kitchen Closet: Coming Out as a Foodie!* In this chapter I describe some of the best foodie websites on the web and where to find really special stuff to serve guests at business or home events. Why shop online? Simple. Today, everybody shops for gourmet foods at their local gourmet food store, but that means everybody is fishing from the same pond. This makes it more difficult to find really special things with which to wow your company. By contrast, there are literally hundreds of fun and exotic foodie websites that you can visit to find exotic items that you'd never find in your local gourmet food shop. Because website URLs change constantly, I recommend that you use my website, www.eddieosterland.com, as the portal to visit all of the foodie websites I talk about in this chapter. That way, you'll enjoy a hassle-free online shopping experience and be eligible for discounts on many online food products.

- *Chapter 9: Power Entertaining at Home.* In Chapter 9 I tell you how to start a wine collection (or wine cellar) and use it as the basis for power entertaining at home. I provide tips on what to include in your wine collection and how and where to store it. I also encourage readers to collect a broad international sampling of wines from various wine-growing regions around the world, including France, Germany, Italy, Spain, Australia, New Zealand, South Africa, South America, and, of course, Washington State, Oregon, California, and New York (especially Long Island).

- *Chapter 10: Masterminds: From Wine Geek to Wine Expert.* Ever thought of turning your hobby and passion for wine into a full-time profession? It's a big leap from wine hobbyist or geek to wine professional, but in this chapter I talk about credentials you may want to pursue to become a sommelier, wine merchant, or wine educator. I discuss the four most esteemed organizations that offer professional wine credentials around the world and how they differ from one another. I wrote this chapter as a public service to my fellow sommeliers and wine educators who undertake extensive education and training to become wine professionals (and who deserve acknowledgment for doing so). I also wrote it for all those who aspire to learn more about the business and scholarly sides of the wine world.

So, there you have it, my friend: an overview of what *Power Entertaining* is all about. You're going to learn a lot about being a power entertainer in the pages that follow. But first, to set the stage for things, let's start in Chapter 2 by talking about what you should *never* do when planning a big business dinner and reception in a hotel. And I mean *never!*

2

Toss (and I Do Mean TOSS) That Caesar Salad!

Never accept a boilerplate hotel menu!

—Eddie O.

If you're like most businesspeople, you've probably spent more time in hotel ballrooms for business dinners than you care to remember. And one reason you'd probably like to forget most of these events is because of the forgettable entrées you were served as a prelude to the evening's speaker (who, in most cases, was probably forgettable, too!).

Maybe it was the chicken Kiev that got trapped in a steam tray for hours before the event and had the consistency of tire rubber by the time you got to take your first bite. Or maybe it was that piece of extremely well-done filet mignon (yes, *that's* what it was!) that tasted more like a hockey puck than a succulent and mouthwatering piece of beef!

So just why *are* hotel business dinners so often lousy and forgettable meals? And why do hotel banquet managers propose the same tired-ass menu options to companies and organizations again and again, even though the track record of these food items in pleasuring people's palates is dubious at best?

You'd think that in an upscale hotel (where room service costs $100 a pop for upscale in-room meals) that the dinner served to people in the ballroom would be as upscale as that served in the best seafood place or steakhouse down the street. But sadly, that is not the case.

Want to know a secret? Most hotels propose the same menu items to business groups again and again for one simple reason: they know what items to propose that will generate the biggest profit margins for *them*. And they presume that you'll defer to their professional culinary judgment. I've seen it happen again and again.

Take Caesar salad, for example—that old warhorse of a salad choice for many business dinners. Hotels push this on people (especially for banquet-sized dinner events) because it's easy to make ahead of time. What's more, it costs hotels just pennies to prepare, while the hotel may gouge your organization up to $7.50 a plate for it. That really adds up when you have a dinner event for 1,500 people!

What about filet mignon? Sounds good, doesn't it? But not so fast!

When purchased by the ton by hotels (not uncommon), it's cheap and can stay in a "hot box" (those Sterno-heated aluminum boxes that are ubiquitous in all banquet kitchens) and not change color for 40 minutes. It's nearly indestructible—just like shoe leather!

So what can you do to avoid serving these tired travelers on hotel plates?

Toss That Caesar Salad Right Now!

The next time you're in an airport, check out the "To Go" items at any of the shops or food stands near your gate. There's a reason why Caesar salad is one of the most common items you see. I call it one of those indestructible, "industrial-strength" meals that you can make, take, sell, and consume anywhere. I'm surprised it's not standard issue in military rations. But do you really want it as part of a business dinner, too?

Recently, a client of mine, an association executive I'll call "John," contacted me for help in preparing a major dinner event he wanted to host for his business colleagues. He wanted to stage something that would be truly memorable for people, something over the top.

"Eddie, my colleagues have been everywhere, and they've seen it all. How do I give them something that will really impress them?"

I asked John to describe the event he had in mind, and it sounded very typical: the group planned to start with a networking reception, which would be followed by a dinner and a dinner speaker. To which I thought, "Oh God, that's so boring!"

After asking him a few questions, I asked him to send me the proposed dinner menu that the hotel had prepared after consulting with him and his staff. And what I saw was appalling! Here's what the hotel proposed:

A Hotel's Standard Offering for the Contractors' Association of America National Meeting

Reception: 6:00 to 7:15

Cocktails

Well items $6.75 per drink; premium brands $9.25
House-brand Chardonnay and Cabernet Sauvignon $7.00 per glass

Hors d'oeuvres

Crudités with ranch and blue cheese dip, imported cheese and fruit platters, pâtés, imported olives, Italian salami, with assorted Grissini crackers, focaccia bread with olive oil and balsamic vinegar

Salad

Caesar salad with garlic croutons

(*continued*)

(*continued*)

Appetizer

Seafood extravaganza: shrimp, Alaskan crab legs, clams, and crispy calamari

Wine

Clos du Bois Napa Chardonnay or Fetzer Sauvignon Blanc

Intermezzo

Green tea sorbet infused with Grey Goose citron

Entrée

Duet of local organic free-range Colorado filet mignon and sustainable wild Alaskan salmon

Wine

Louis Martini Cabernet Sauvignon or Pinot Noir

Dessert

Chocolate mousse cake with warm Ghirardelli chocolate sauce

Now, I bet you're thinking, "Eddie, wait a minute! You say this menu is horrible? It looks pretty good to me. I've had that menu. In fact, I've had that menu again and again and again."

Which is *precisely* my point!

This menu is boilerplate, *and* it's boring! It gets served at business dinners in hotel ballrooms across the United States every night. There's nothing original or creative about it.

What's more, it's priced to make the hotel a hefty profit, not to make dinner guests happy or to please their palates.

After I had reviewed the proposed hotel menu, I called John and told him what I thought. Following is a portion of the critique I offered him.

The Reception

For starters, I told John that the reception, as the hotel envisioned it, was far too long. Scheduled to go from 6:00 PM to 7:15 PM, I saw it as little more than an excuse for people to get hammered ahead of the speaker and dinner event to follow.

"You know what people do at a reception like this, John?" I asked him. "They walk in with their best friend, park themselves near the bar, graze on mixed nuts, and chat for 45 minutes. They don't move around and network with other people. Nobody does!" I went on to tell him that by the time dinner was served, people would be so lit that they wouldn't taste (much less remember) anything about the evening.

Next, I offered a few choice words about the wine selection. I told him it showed no imagination at all, but again, would reap a giant windfall for the hotel. "John, what the hotel is proposing here is a gold mine for them but will cost you a Saudi prince's ransom."

I told John that for the kind of event he wanted, a hotel typically purchases 1,000 cases of wine then marks the bottles up 500 percent!

I suggested to John that he ask to see the hotel's full wine list. Better yet, I said, "Consider purchasing and bringing your *own* wine and paying the corkage charge. That way you'll know you're getting a good wine and won't be getting gouged for it!"

The Hors d'Oeuvres

We then discussed the hors d'oeuvres. The hotel was proposing carrots and celery sticks as well as a selection of fruit and cheese (wheels of Brie and Camembert and wedges of blue cheese with assorted nuts). The carrots and celery sticks might be okay for a Weight Watchers' Convention but *not* for John's crowd. I knew his group would want something more substantial. As for the fruit and cheese, I told John that although it's popular, fruit and wine really don't mix that well. "The stuff the hotel is proposing to you might be tasty fare, but none of it goes with wine," I explained.

"So, what kind of cheese *does* go with wine?" John asked, almost desperate at this point for some good news.

"Cheeses that flatter wine should be of the hard-rind type," I explained. "This includes cheeses such as Pecorino, Parmesan, Manchego, and aged Gouda."

"Ohhh . . . ," he said.

I went on to explain to John that if you slather Brie, which is 80 percent butterfat, on your palate, it coats your tongue with so much fat that you won't be able to taste the wine. As for bread served with olive oil (another hotel suggestion), "It fills you up with useless calories and deadens your appetite—the complete opposite of what you're trying to achieve!"

"I see." John was starting to get it.

The Entrée

Having savaged the hotel's suggestions for the reception, I next went on to attack the hotel's choice of entrée: a "duet" of filet mignon and wild Alaskan salmon. Sounds upscale doesn't it? Packed with protein, too, right? Well, call it what you like— "Reef & Beef" or "Surf & Turf"—serving this duet of fish and beef on the same plate is *unconscionable*, in my view. And I told John as much.

"Why?" he asked.

"Well, for starters, comingling a bloody steak on the same plate with fish juices is a gastronomic nightmare. The flavors will be competing with each other, not complementing each other," I explained. "For some reason, though, the average American thinks these two make a classy pair. They don't!"

"I see," he said.

I went on to explain that the hotel's choice of filet mignon really was not that surprising. "When purchased in bulk, a hotel can mark it up significantly for service to large banquet groups and pocket a nice profit," I told John. Moreover, I explained that although it *can* be a delectable entrée when ordered in a restaurant, when served en masse to hundreds or thousands of dinner guests at a hotel banquet, it can wind up tasting like shoe leather (or a hockey puck) after lurking for hours in a hot box.

"Well, I certainly don't want that," said John, a mischievous smile now dawning like sunshine on his face. John was clearly beginning to see the lay of the land here.

After panning all of the hotel's suggestions for the evening, I said, "John, let me create a menu that people *will* remember you for. In fact, I'll create *more* than a meal; I'll create an event for the evening. You'll be happy I did!"

"Please do," he said.

And so I did. Here it is. (Drum roll please):

Eddie Osterland's *"Quest for the Best!"* Menu for the Contractors' Association of America National Meeting

Reception: 6:00 to 7:00

Passport to the Wines and Foods of the World

Setting: On an outdoor terrace, there are five stations representing some of the major wine-growing regions of the world. Each station features a "magnetic" food and wine combination from France, California, Spain, Italy, and Germany. Guests are issued a "passport" designed to guide them through their taste adventure destinations.

First Course

Smoked sturgeon rillettes, house-made brioche and tangerine caviar sauce

Wines

New World versus Old World comparison of one the greatest "food wines" on the planet: Sauvignon Blanc

(continued)

(*continued*)

Wines to Be Sampled

2007 Didier Dagueneau Pouilly Fume "Pur Sang" from Sancerre, France
2007 Rochioli Estate Sauvignon Blanc Russian River Valley, Sonoma, California

Entrée

Sous vide Kobe Wagyu beef cheeks
Includes:

> Salsify (European herb root) with guanciale bacon (unsmoked Italian bacon prepared with pig's jowl or cheeks—mouthwatering)
>
> Morel and black trumpet mushroom strudel with ramps (bulbous herbs of the Lily family, including the onion, garlic, chive, leek, and shallot)
>
> Sheep's milk ricotta gnocchi

Wines

A vintage comparison tasting of one of Napa Valley's most elegant wines: Corison Cabernet Sauvignon

> Vintage 2006
>
> Vintage 2001 (Released only for us this evening, this wine is one of the most elegant, silky Cabernets ever made in Napa Valley.)

Salade

Simple chilled Romaine and Mâche (lamb's lettuce) with light shallot vinaigrette
Artisanal cheese selections:

Goat: Consider Bardwell Manchester (Vermont, USA)
Cow: Meadow Creek Grayson (Virginia, USA)
Sheep: Roquefort d'Argental (Midi, France)

Dessert

Warm sabayon custard with 15-year old Blandy's Malmsey Madeira

A day or so after I e-mailed this menu proposal to John, he called me. "Eddie, this is more than I could ever have imagined. People will talk about this event forever. They'll say, *Remember when John* . . ."

"I told you so," I said.

After making a few more suggestions to John, I worked with him and his organization to help put his event on. In my role as sommelier, I offered "between courses" comments to the guests to acquaint them with what they were eating and with how various menu items were designed to work together in culinary harmony. I'm happy to say that the event was a blowout success. In fact, people at John's organization are still talking about this event to this very day, more than five years later. It was truly a night to remember.

So, you may be wondering, what other advice did I give John before we actually put on his event?

Here it is: whenever you're planning a big business event with a social dimension to it—be it for customers, prospects, or business associates—you have to do it right. And, if you want it to be memorable for people, you also have to think *out of the box*. This doesn't necessarily mean spending more money, but it does involve thinking in new ways about how you host people, make them feel comfortable, and entice them to do business with you and your company or organization.

Here are the specific things I recommend you do to make *your* business events, both successful and novel. Think of these recommendations as Eddie's Checklist of things to do if you ever have to organize and manage a large social or banquet event in a hotel for business associates or clients. Do them well, and people will talk about your event for weeks, if not for years!

Eddie's Checklist for Planning, Managing, and Hosting Flawless Banquet Events

At the Reception

- ☐ Never give people time to have more than two drinks, or you'll lose them for the rest of the evening. For that reason, limit the reception to no more than an hour, tops!
- ☐ Get a mixologist to create a signature cocktail custom-designed for your event and give it a catchy name. For example, I once took 10 people to an Alan Parsons concert in San Diego, California, and had Fred Dexheimer, a top New York City mixologist, design a cocktail called, "Eye in the Sky," named after Parsons's most famous song. Everyone loved it!
- ☐ To get people to actually mingle and network at your reception, have the hotel set up four or five stations in different parts of the room. At each station, serve tested wine and food combinations that are *magnetic*—that really pop. You'll have to do some research on this (see Chapter 4 for ideas), but it's worth it because if it's done right, you'll own people's palates and they will adore you! People will be eager to move around to sample the other delicacies you are featuring in other parts of the room.
- ☐ At the start of your event, announce the presence of the food stations to your guests and encourage them to visit each one.
- ☐ Serve your initial wine to people before you serve them much food. Why? Appetites are fragile. You want to excite people with wines they've never tried, and when people are a little bit hungry, it makes the latent flavors and textures in wines pop on the palate. This is when the glory of a good wine really comes through, before it is dulled by a totally satisfied appetite!

When It Comes to Entrées

☐ Choose unfamiliar entrées, as suggested in my revised menu. For example, serve smoked sturgeon rillettes and Wagyu beef cheeks cooked sous vide. Sturgeon melts better than butter in your mouth, and cheeks of any kind (halibut, hamachi, veal) are exotic and wonderful. Cooking them sous vide (in vacuum bags at a very low temperature for a very long time) is all the rage with today's chefs and gourmet home cooks.

☐ During dinner, serve wines in pairs. Serving two wines in side-by-side comparisons throughout the meal adds an educational dimension to your dinner. It gets people talking to one another, too. For example, you could serve the same grapes from two different countries (the United States and France) during the appetizer course. Then, you might serve two of the same wines from vintages five years apart during the entrée course. In the latter case, tasting the two wines at the same time shows how much of a difference age makes.

Vegetable Dishes: Will You Be Boring or Adventurous and Provocative?

☐ Most vegetable dishes that hotels suggest are really boring. Why? Hotels do what's easiest and most profitable for them. In the menu I recommended to John, I suggested a wonderful European vegetable called salsify, which has a scrumptious, edible root similar to a parsnip. Most people have never tried this wonderful root veggie.

☐ In the sample menu in this chapter, I also suggested morels and black trumpet mushrooms. These are very expensive and almost never seen in hotels, but their flavor comes across like mushrooms on steroids. You almost jump when you taste them.

☐ Meat entrées enjoy bonding with some form of starch. Most hotels answer this with garlic mashed potatoes. As a creative alternative, I recommend gnocchi (Italian thick, soft dumplings) served with sheep's milk ricotta cheese. This is still *comfort food*, but it is uncontrollably exuberant. It explodes in your mouth!

☐ Don't allow banquet managers to include $6 shrimps or other superexpensive appetizers in your banquet order. It's not worth it.

☐ Also, don't buy large predinner salads or an intermezzo course. These options fill people up and often can cost you a bundle.

Salade Course

☐ As noted earlier, banish Caesar salad from your menu! As I said, hotels push these on everyone because they can make a lot of money selling them to you en masse. But they are nothing special. If you really want to serve a salad, do it like the French and Italians do. Serve a lightly dressed salade *after* the entrée—to help people digest their meals. Try chilled Romaine and Mache leaves dressed with shallot vinaigrette. (Avoid balsamic vinaigrette, as it is way too strong and will overwhelm the lettuce.)

☐ Ask the hotel caterers to guarantee that the plates and salad are served ice cold.

☐ Finally, understand the real role a salad is supposed to play in a meal. The French say that *"la salade est pour dégraisser."* Translated, that means a salad's purpose is to degrease your palate and help food settle in your stomach.

Gourmet Cheese Course

☐ The cheese course of a meal can be fun and eye-opening. And it gives you a great chance to introduce your guests to some new players on the cheese board beyond basic cheddars and Brie.

☐ Where can you find fine cheeses? If you don't have a local gourmet cheese store near you, I suggest calling Murray's Cheese in New York City. Ask for their resident cheesemonger. When I last spoke with Murray's, they suggested three types of cheeses for meals from three different sources: goats, cows, and sheep. You can order their cheeses (and others) online—which is how I buy most food items these days. They will deliver them overnight in perfect condition.

☐ Serve all cheeses at room temperature. Hotel caterers tend to bring cheese straight from the refrigerator, but that should never be allowed. Hotels do the same thing with ice cream and serve it hard as a rock. When I worked at Hôtel de la Poste in France, they had one person whose sole job was to ensure that everything went out to people's tables at the right temperature (butter, ice cream, foie gras terrine, and cheese).

Light Dessert Course

☐ People are usually so full by the end of the meal that they only sample what's served for dessert, often a chocolate something-or-other. Instead, serve up sabayon, extremely light warm custard often made with Marsala wine. Or, for something extra special, make it with Madeira. Madeira is one of the most fascinating wines in the world. If you turn your guests on to this wine, you'll secure their friendship forever!

Now, Give People Something to Take Home with Them

☐ No, I'm not talking about doggie bags! I'm talking about giving your guests a memento of their evening with you: a copy of the over-the-top medley of wine and food you've just served them, for example. Print the menu of the evening, including all food items, wines/vintages, and recipes for the meal, on small, 4 × 6-inch cards that people can put in their pocket or purse. Doing this will help people remember the evening and enable them to replicate the menu at a later date for their own function. They'll thank you for this!

☐ If you don't do this, your guests aren't likely to remember the wine, vintage, cocktail, and food items they enjoyed at your event. And that would be a pity, indeed.

Chapter Wrap-Up

So there you have it, my friend! Just a few things to keep in mind when planning a big business event at a hotel near you. I'll have a lot more to say about this in other chapters.

Remember, your goal in hosting *any* big business or client event is to impress people and give them an experience they'll long remember. Treat people with generosity and old-world hospitality, and they *will* remember it—for a long time. It will set you apart from the competition. And in today's world, that really counts. After all, we all know courtesy and hospitality are in pretty short supply these days!

Treating people well is good for business; it helps nurture and cement relationships. The goodwill, friendships, relationships, and repeat business that come from entertaining with class and panache can be incredible. And besides, who doesn't enjoy being wined and dined once in a while?

With that, I offer a toast: "*A votre santé!*" (which in French means "To your health!"). Let's move now to Chapter 3, "20 Secrets of Successful Power Entertaining."

3

20 Secrets of Successful Power Entertaining

Position yourself as a center of influence—the one who knows the movers and shakers. People will respond to that, and you'll soon become what you project.
—Bob Burg
Author, *Endless Referrals:*
Network Your Everyday Contacts into Sales

As I noted in Chapter 1, a lot of business entertaining today still relies on tired, outdated methods of getting people together so that they can make connections, network with one another, sell to one another, and build business relationships. A further fact is that these methods aren't just tired and boring; they're often ineffective and even unproductive from a cost/benefit standpoint.

Consider all the dollars that companies spend to host booths at industry trade shows but that often fail to generate even one or two really good qualified sales leads! Or consider the typical business networking reception at a hotel that includes lots of boozing, lots of schmoozing, and lots of loud talk in a crowded hotel suite. (You've been to a hundred of these events over the years, I'm sure.) These events give attendees lots of opportunity to "gain personal altitude" while ostensibly doing "business development." But be honest, how many times have you been to such networking events only to realize the next day that you drank too much, ate too many peanuts, didn't collect anybody's business card, and can't even remember the names of the people you schmoozed with for a couple of hours in a crowded room?

There's got to be a better way to network with people—and to build connections with clients and business prospects—than this, right?

You bet there is, and the way to do it is by using power entertaining principles and practices to plan and host enjoyable and memorable business events.

Remember, power entertaining is about creating an experience for guests; an experience built around great wine, great food, great company, and great ambience. It's about giving people enjoyable memories that, when they look back, will cause them to remember you fondly and make them want to do business with you in the future!

So here are 20 power entertaining tips to help you take your business entertaining to a new level. Think of these as my secrets (based on my years of experience as a Master Sommelier) about how to throw a successful party—albeit a party with a business purpose. Employ these principles anytime you need to put on a business event with a social dimension, regardless of its size, scope, or purpose. They'll help you forge lasting relationships with clients and business colleagues. And, they'll ensure you put on events that clients, prospects, friends, and even your boss will talk about for days—or weeks—afterward!

My 20 Secrets of Successful Power Entertaining

Tip #1: Think of Power Entertaining as a Business Development Strategy

You can brand yourself (and your company) with others by creating memorable and enjoyable social events that people will long remember and always associate with *you!* Hosting power entertaining events is a great way, as Bob Burg suggests in this chapter's opening quote, to become "a center of influence" in your business, industry niche, or marketplace. That's because every event you put on for others is an opportunity to create an indelible impression— *a special moment*—in the minds of others. Even tired and jaded businesspeople who attend a lot of business networking events enjoy social gatherings that feature a festive atmosphere, a few surprises, warm hospitality, good food, and the opportunity to enjoy the company of others.

Creating an enjoyable and memorable experience for other people doesn't need to bust your food and entertainment budget, either. The goal of power entertaining events isn't to provide people with a Vegas-style all-night, all-you-can-eat buffet, even though you might think this if you go to some business functions! Instead, power entertaining is about offering people *delectable samples of food and tastings of wine*, especially of things they haven't had before or don't know much about. Events are built around enjoyable wine and food pairings offered to people either in a reception-style or intimate dinner format.

Tip #2: Be an Enthusiastic Master of Ceremonies at Your Events!

Power entertaining is about making others feel special at business events you host. It's therefore important to dive into your hosting role with gusto, extending the welcome mat to people as they arrive, exuding warmth and hospitality, setting the tone for why people are together, and describing what the evening is all about. If you decide to have a "theme" for the evening—for example, "Select Wines of the New World/Old World"—share this with attendees and explain the fun way people will be introduced to different wines and foods over the course of their evening together.

To prepare for your social responsibilities as a power entertainer, consider taking a wine and food course to learn more about the culinary arts and the finer points of entertaining others. Courses are available in most communities across the country and can provide you with an excellent layperson's knowledge of wine and of how to host social events with knowledge, ease, charm, and confidence. For information on finding courses in your community, visit www.local wineevents.com.

Tip #3: Engage a Sommelier or Wine Merchant to Help You Plan and Host Events

A sommelier or wine merchant will be very knowledgeable about wine and will be able to help you design unique wine and food pairings to feature at your dinner or reception (see Chapter 5). You may also want to retain a caterer and engage your corporate support staff to coordinate event logistics, develop invitation lists, send invitations, and determine specific menus, timing, and other details.

Tip #4: Design Your Menu with the Goal of Introducing Guests to Wines and Foods They're Not Familiar With

At many corporate events the only alcoholic beverages people serve are cheap, garden-variety brands of Chardonnay, Cabernet, or Merlot. It's the same boring stuff you'd find in any hotel minibar or on any short-haul domestic airline flight! So why not be more imaginative? Instead of everyday Chardonnay and Merlot, offer people Sauvignon Blanc (Sancerre), Tempranillo (Rioja), Sangiovese (Chianti), and other wines that go well with specific foods. (For more, see Chapter 4.)

Tip #5: Kick the Evening off with Champagne!

Before serving people *any* food, start by giving them champagne or sparking wine as they arrive. Most Americans associate champagne and sparkling wine only with special occasions such as birthdays, weddings, graduations, and New Year's Eve. But in my opinion, it's something exquisite that people should enjoy much more often than that. So consider greeting guests at future social events with a tray full of crystal flutes of nice bubbly. People feel instantly special when you do this. It delights and dazzles them—and what a first impression it makes!

Although great French champagne (from Champagne, France) is expensive—costing upward of $60 to $120 a bottle—you can offer people less expensive alternatives such as Cava from Spain. These will cost you between $10 and $18 a bottle, even less if you buy them by the case. Spend serious money on great French champagne only when you know your guests would recognize the difference. Not many will!

Tip #6: Serve People Your Best Stuff First

Ever enjoyed a night of dining in a three-star restaurant in France? On arrival, the waiter or waitress typically brings you an extraordinarily scrumptious little morsel of something the French call an *amuse-gueule*, or palate tickler. It's always a hit with guests because people are so hungry when they first arrive that downing this tiny tidbit makes a hugely positive impression. The French, who are masters of entertaining and the culinary arts, know this. So they give diners what is arguably the best thing they'll have all night at the beginning of the evening. It then sets the tone for the entire meal to come.

You should do the same thing at power entertaining events. Most people will arrive for your event coming from work, and perhaps after running around at the office all day. They're likely to be famished. So instead of offering them mixed nuts, pretzels, raw vegetables, and potato chips like everybody else does, serve them small sampler portions of foods like Ventresca, which is delightfully scrumptious tuna belly from Spain and Italy; Scottish smoked salmon; foie gras; or, perhaps my favorite appetizer of all, *jamón ibérico de bellota*, a kind of Spanish ham that looks like prosciutto but is far more exotic. This ham comes from a pig that is either grain- or acorn-fed for the last three months of its life. It has a unique fat content that melts at room temperature, giving the ham a distinct nuttiness that most people have never experienced. It is ravishingly scrumptious!

Tip #7: Serve Wines in Pairs

I recommend that you design power entertaining events around side-by-side comparisons of different wines at various points throughout the evening. Doing this adds an intellectual dimension to your event or dinner party. It can also be a lot of fun, both for you and your guests. Wine pairings can take many forms. You could, for example, do a side-by-side blind comparison of a good wine

($15 a bottle) and a very good wine ($35 a bottle) and see how people distinguish the flavor of one from the other. Or you could serve a Cabernet from France and one from California to illustrate how geography influences winemaking styles and taste. Or you could serve up the same wine from two different vintages (years) to demonstrate the significance of vintage variation to a wine's flavor. Do two to four side-by-side comparisons of wines throughout an evening (followed by complementary food items and/or dinner courses), moving from reds to whites to dessert wines.

Serving two wines simultaneously and giving people a chance to do side-by-side comparisons of what they're tasting isn't just educational; it also melts the ice and helps people mingle. I've done these pairings hundreds of times with groups of different sizes, and it injects a whole new social dimension into an evening, as people ponder what they've tasted and chat about it with their fellow guests. Doing such comparisons is also a great way to broaden people's taste repertoires, and they will thank you for this at the end of the evening because you're giving them something tangible that they can take back and share with their own friends and colleagues! (For more on wine pairings, see Chapters 4 and 6).

Tip #8: Do Side-By-Side Comparisons of Food, Too

Use the concept of side-by-side comparisons for food as well as for wines and introduce your guests to new food discoveries. For example, give people a chance to taste three different varieties of the Spanish ham *jamón ibérico* that I mentioned earlier. Three different varieties of this ham—*serrano*, *ibérico*, and *ibérico de bellota*—are available, so you could do side-by-side comparisons of each type (which vary in their fat content) so that people get a sense of what they're paying for in each case. Or do a side-by-side tasting of a cheese at different ages. You could have people taste a young Parmesan cheese (6 months old) next to an old Parmesan (18 months) and a very old Parmesan (30 months). Do comparison tastings like this, and you'll be introducing people to the incredible evolution of flavors and textures that occurs in the cheese aging process.

Tip #9: Learn about Food Wines

One of the most important, but often overlooked, attributes that certain wines offer is their ability to enhance food flavors. When enjoyed to their fullest (not just as beverages), these wines can play the role of a condiment to food, much the same as salt, pepper, and a lemon slice do on a piece of fish. Food wines have the ability to amplify food flavors thanks to their elevated levels of acidity. Some of the best white food wines include Sauvignon Blancs from France, New Zealand, South Africa, and California and dry Rieslings from Germany, Australia, Austria, California, and Washington State. Some of the best red food wines include Barbera from Italy; Cabernet Franc from France and California; Pinot Noir from California, Oregon, France, and New Zealand; Sangiovese from Italy; and Tempranillo from Spain.

Tip #10: Teach Guests the Concept of Wine and Food Synergy

$1 + 1 = 3$ is the business formula that represents synergy. Simply stated, when wine is tasted with the right foods, the combined flavors are better than if each item were tasted separately. People often eat their food and then wash it down with wine. Teach your guests not to see wine just as a beverage but as a condiment and complement to fine food. You'll be teaching them something very subtle and special.

Tip #11: Always Warm Your Whites and Chill Your Reds before Serving Them

Yes, I know this runs counter to most people's thinking, but you want to guard against overchilling your white wines and serving your red wines too warm. White wines are often served too cold, especially in the United States. However, a white wine's subtle aromatics (floral and fruity notes) are anesthetized at refrigerator temperatures. So take your white wines out of the refrigerator about 20 minutes before you want to serve them.

Conversely, red wines often are not served chilled enough. Their "finish" can thus be a bit harsh, even caustic to the taste, if served at room temperature. To remove this edge, chill your red wines for about 20 minutes before you want to serve them to guests. This will give them the proper balance and fruit intensity when served. To help you maintain the proper temperatures of your wines, you may want to invest in a digital wine thermometer. The proper temperature for whites is about 50 degrees Fahrenheit and for reds, about 65 degrees Fahrenheit. (More about this in Chapter 7.)

Tip #12: Be Classy and Decant Your Reds

Decanting a red wine allows it to open up and breathe. Allow at least an hour for this. Decanting also allows you to pour your wine off of its sediment. Using a decanter contributes the added ingredient of "theater" to your power entertaining event. A company called Riedel (pronounced "Reedle") makes the best decanters around.

Tip #13: As a Power Entertainer, Invest in the Right "Power Tools" to Add Drama to Your Events

No, I'm not talking here about hammers and saws and screwdrivers. But in keeping with the theme and principles of power entertaining it's important that you invest in some special bartending accessories to add panache, style, and flourish to the power entertaining events you put on and host. Using these tools adds an element of color, theater, and excitement to your events and helps set you apart from everybody else who does business entertaining. Here's a list of what you need to have and/or do:

- *Buy classy glassware.* Very few people or organizations have elegant wine glasses, so go out and buy at least a dozen nice red wine glasses and a dozen nice white wine glasses, as well as a set of 12 champagne flutes. Personally, I recommend *The One* stemware line, developed by Andrea Robinson, a fellow Master Sommelier. These European-style glasses have been custom engineered to optimize the aroma and taste of both red and white wines. Moreover, they are break-resistant, dishwasher-safe, and half the cost of other European crystal stems. In addition to these glasses, you may want to invest in some Riedel Sommelier Burgundy and Montrachet glasses for special occasions.

One note about the care of nice stemware: in many cases, you'll have professional kitchen or hotel staff washing stemware for you after an event. When hosting a power entertaining event at home, though it's another matter. If you are washing up at home, wait to wash your fine crystal glassware until the morning *after* your event. You'll lower your "kill rate" on glasses by 20 percent! Once washed, polish your glasses with a microfiber cloth (no lint) to remove water spots before putting them away.

- *Buy a nice decanter or two (or three).* As noted, decanters are a classy way to prepare red wine for serving ahead of time. You can spend literally hundreds of dollars for these, but you don't need to. Buy one that you can afford and consult a sommelier or wine merchant about what makes the most sense for you.

- *Buy a wine aerator and use it if you don't have time to decant red wines.* Using these devices helps oxygenate a wine to improve its aromatics. There are numerous models out there. Vinturi makes an excellent model.

- *Get a digital wine thermometer.* As noted earlier, this important tool assists you in making sure that the wines you serve are at proper temperatures.

- *Have a nice wine opener on hand.* Lots of good wine openers are available, both expensive and inexpensive. For my money, one of the best inexpensive wine openers you can buy is the Quick Click wine opener, which costs about $15. If you want something more upscale, consider the Code 38 product line of wine openers. Truly the Rolls-Royce of wine openers, these professional grade tools, used by many of the world's top sommeliers, are exquisitely designed and engineered, and they can cost as much as a magnum of high-end wine. All the wine openers mentioned above are available on my website, www.eddieoster land.com.

- *Purchase one or more wine refrigerators to keep your wines ready for service at all times.* Wine refrigerators are a great piece of equipment to own as part of power entertaining and doing it right. Sub-Zero makes some the best wine refrigerators on the market. (More about wine refrigerators in Chapter 9.)

- *Purchase plastic wine bottle insulators/coolers.* Wine insulators (by the way, they don't chill wines) have a thermal-paned jacket of air that surrounds your wine and keeps it at proper temperature for more than an hour. You'll need one of these for each bottle of wine you want to serve to a group. Buy at least two so you can do side-by-side comparisons.

- *Consider buying a luxury wine dispenser such as the EuroCave SoWine Home Wine Bar.* Having one of these units around will impress your friends and add class to any home entertaining function. Designed by the EuroCave Company of Lyon, France, these dispensers allow you to keep two bottles in two independent compartments (46 to 50 degrees Fahrenheit for the whites and 61 to 65 degrees Fahrenheit for the reds) and to serve both kinds of wine at an ideal temperature.

Tip #14: Become Knowledgeable about Wine and Food Etiquette

As a Master Sommelier, I was trained in the fine art of wine, hospitality, and service, and many of the lessons and best practices I've learned and practiced over the years are things you should be aware of, too, when entertaining others. Anyone can become a successful "host," and with the knowledge of food and wine you'll gain from reading this book, you'll be able to power entertain with confidence in a wide variety of business situations.

Tip #15: As the Host, Stay Attentive to the Needs of Your Guests throughout the Evening

Too often I've been to business events where the designated "host" of the evening didn't do a very good job of mingling with others, introducing guests to one another, and making everyone in attendance feel special. This is more important than you can imagine. Many people dread the thought of going to business events that involve a social component. And many people get nervous when entering a room full of people they don't know or don't know well. Surprisingly, even very senior-level people may be ill at ease when around others in social situations. Be conscious of this as you organize power entertaining events and make efforts when hosting events to help people mingle. If necessary, enlist others (colleagues or direct reports) to help you with this.

Tip #16: Give People Souvenirs to Take Home

As I said in Chapter 2, I'm not talking doggie bags here. But I am talking about giving your guests a nice take-home souvenir of their evening with you. For example, when I prepare menus for power entertaining events, I often put the pairings of food and wine together on glossy 4×6 cards so that people can replicate the same wine and food pairings with their own clients (or at home) if they like. And when I do my Passport to the Wines of the World receptions (www .eddieosterland.com), I often print my menu and wine selections for the event on paper stock that looks like an actual passport. It sounds corny, but people love this stuff. And it will cause them to remember you well after the event has passed!

Tip #17: Learn the Finer Points of Wine Service

For example, use finesse if opening wine bottles yourself. Many people, including many restaurant waiters, often mutilate the top of wine bottles as they open them. Avoid this by cutting the wine capsule (the metal shrouded top of the bottle) carefully just below the lip so as not to ruin the integrity of the capsule. Then proceed to extract the cork.

Tip #18: Don't Forget the Sound, Light, and Magic

No power entertaining event is complete without paying a little attention to stagecraft. I'm a big believer that hosting events should include music, maybe some mood lighting, if feasible, and a good sound system if you're going to play music and/or host a large event. For very large events, you'll also want to arrange for a wireless lavalier mic to help you be heard as host over the din! Play CDs or MP3 music selections between wine and food servings. This adds festivity to the air. Don't let the music be too loud; you want to encourage conversation among people. I like to play soft jazz and instrumentals.

Tip #19: Learn How to Work with Restaurants to Plan Events

It's very likely that, from time to time, you'll want to work closely with restaurants to plan and host events. I cover this topic in depth in Chapter 5, but in general here are things to keep in mind when working with restaurants:

- *Know the wine list and menu.* Both are usually on a restaurant's website. If not, call the restaurant and ask them to e-mail these to you.
- *Work with the restaurant's sommelier to design the wine and food menu for your event.*
- *To get good service from a restaurant, plan on tipping generously in cash at the front end (before the event itself).* This is called front-loading. Plan on tipping at least 20 percent of the final estimated cost for the event. And consider a tip of 25 percent to secure the best and most enthusiastic service possible from the sommelier/captain and wait staff.

Tip #20: Use the Element of Surprise to Delight and Dazzle People

Being a power entertainer is, in large part, about delighting others. So find ways to incorporate elements of drama, suspense, and surprise into your power entertaining events. This will make the events you host fun, memorable, and sometimes unforgettable. When I say surprise people, I mean it, too! As my friend and fellow professional speaker Mikki Williams puts it: "Be outrageous; it's the only place that isn't crowded!" A few years ago I took Mikki's advice personally when I threw an outrageous surprise birthday party for myself (see sidebar).

I Love Being Outrageous!

I love a great party, so a few years ago, when I reached a certain "milestone birthday," I decided to throw myself a surprise birthday party—except I didn't really do it for myself. Instead, I did it for eight of my closest friends, all of whom are big party lovers and major foodies. I wanted to surprise them with something special, and I succeeded!

Things got rolling one Saturday afternoon when I picked everybody up at their homes in a stretch limo that I'd hired for the occasion. Everybody was dressed up because I'd told them we were going someplace special for dinner. So imagine their surprise when, once in the limo, I offered everybody pink champagne out of a brown paper bag and Ritz crackers with Cheese Whiz on them. Because they'd arrived hungry (per my request) they chomped and swilled away not sure if they'd be getting anything else to eat that evening!

I took them on a short tour of some of San Diego's greasy spoon restaurants, stopping at several to confirm that we did not have dinner reservations at any of them. They were all quite baffled at this, as they knew (hoped) we wouldn't be having dinner in any of these places. But they played along to see what would happen next.

Soon we wound up at the San Diego Airport on a secluded stretch of tarmac alongside a private plane I had waiting for us. (Yes, I was able to arrange this!) I told my friends that I hadn't liked any of the restaurants we'd been to, so we were flying out of town for dinner.

"Where?" somebody asked.

"How does San Francisco sound?" I replied.

My guests boarded the plane, and as they did, I gifted each of them a pair of wireless headphones. As the plane taxied for takeoff, I broke out a couple of magnums of Taittinger Comtes de Champagne (1996) and gave each of them

(continued)

(continued)

a 2-ounce jar of caviar. I also cranked up "Games People Play" by the Alan Parsons Project for people to listen to, as both the plane (and my guests) began to gain altitude. Looking around the cabin at that point I could see everybody was having a great time. After all, just moments before they'd been noshing on Ritz crackers and sipping cheap champagne in the back of a rented limo.

After about an hour, somebody realized we weren't headed to San Francisco. I then fessed up, saying, "I just said, 'How does San Francisco sound'? We're not going there, baby. . . . This is my birthday . . . We're going to Vegas!"

A short time later we landed in Vegas, where we were met by a so-called point man, somebody I'd arranged for ahead of time (courtesy of my friend, philanthropist, and restaurateur Barbara Lazaroff) to help squire us around Vegas over the course of the next six hours. And then we were off! First to the Tao (one of the hippest Pan Asian nightclubs in Vegas) for drinks. That was followed by a five-star dinner at the chef's table at Postrio (where menu items were flown in just for my dinner), all capped by front row seats for an out-of-this-world performance by Cirque du Soleil and postperformance drinks and carrying on at a place that is best left unnamed.

By 3:00 AM Sunday morning we were all at the Vegas airport, and by 6:00 AM I was dropping my now exhausted but thoroughly delighted guests back at their homes in the La Jolla hills.

Now that, my friends, was a party I'll long remember! A party that my friends still talk about to this day. A bit extravagant and outrageous perhaps, but then again I'm a guy who likes to do stuff out of the box! By the way, there's a "class photo" of our Vegas party in the back of this book.

So what might you do to make that next power entertaining event of yours a night to remember?

Chapter Wrap-Up

The 20 Secrets of Successful Power Entertaining I've outlined in this chapter are what I like to call a new operating system for entertaining colleagues, customers, and business prospects with greater style, panache, and polish than they've ever been exposed to before.

But power entertaining is more than just a set of guidelines for doing business entertaining in new ways. It can, in a very real sense, be an extension of your current marketing and business development efforts and give your clients and prospects a very positive "brand experience" of you, your firm, and your commitment to building and sustaining a strong business relationship with them.

4

Power Pairing Great Foods with Great Wines

When pairing wine and food properly, each should accentuate the other's assets.
—Eddie O.

Power couples. When you hear that term you probably think of Brad and Angelina, Beyoncé and Jay-Z, Michele and Barack, or Bill and Hillary!

But in this chapter I want to talk about power couples of another kind: dynamic team-ups that play a big role in power entertaining events and that can be the true "stars" of any evening, if you plan things right.

I'm talking, of course, about the dramatic pairings of food and wine that should be the centerpiece of every power entertaining function you host, because they are a surefire way to delight and engage your guests—almost as if a celebrity *did* show up!

In this chapter you'll learn how to design food and wine couplings *so* scrumptious that they will blow your guests' taste buds away and keep people talking about your event for days! You'll also learn about an important principle I call wine and food synergy.

Food and wine pairings are something that leading restaurants around the world do to delight their guests, and it's a big reason they develop lasting reputations and have such loyal clients. They're something *you* can do as well. And in doing them, you'll brand your business events as something truly special!

Typically, you'll do three or four pairings of wine and food during a 2- or 3-hour power entertaining event. And because they form the very heart of a power entertaining reception or dinner, you'll want to be sure they're planned well ahead of time and also well managed in *real time* for everybody to enjoy.

Pairing good wine and good food is not a random thing; it requires attention to detail, artfulness in choosing items to pair, and attention to what the audience of the evening is likely to enjoy. It also calls for some showmanship on your part and a desire to create an enjoyable and impactful experience for your guests.

Create Wine and Food Synergy

When I design a power entertaining event for clients, I like to pay attention to what I call food and wine synergy. In essence, this means picking pairings of food and wine that, when combined, add up to a sum greater than their parts. Food and wine synergy is a pivotal element in creating good power pairings of food and wine.

You already know something about the synergy that certain flavors have when they're put together. Take, for example, when you're out for dinner at your favorite seafood restaurant and you order swordfish. What's the first thing you do when your order arrives? Most people squeeze a little lemon on their fish to enhance its flavor. That's because the acid in the lemon helps amplify the flavor of the fish. It cuts through any oiliness and, if the fish is not overdone, enhances the fish's flavor. You know this based on your experience and on what you know your palate likes.

Synergy of food and wine works the same way. If you choose carefully, wine can serve the same function with food that a piece of lemon does with fish: it enhances the flavor of the food it is served with and vice versa. In some cases the wine you choose will be white; in other cases, red. The object is to choose something that amplifies the flavors of the food you are serving, something that acts as a "stunt double" for the lemon and leads to an out-of-this-world taste experience for anyone who tastes the food and wine pair simultaneously. If you do this artfully, you'll create unforgettable combinations of great food and wine. In fact, you'll have people eating out of your hand every time you throw a business function!

In the case of the swordfish I described previously, you need a crisp wine (red or white) that has the requisite acidity to fire up the flavors and cut through buttery or creamy sauces. But in other cases, with a piece of lamb or pork, for example, you'll want an entirely different kind of wine. (Take a look at the sidebar for examples of some truly classic wine and food pairings.)

These Dance Partners Were Made for Each Other

Champagne and Caviar

What a pair these two make! The rich "moussey" consistency of champagne balances off the brininess of caviar quite nicely. The bubbles also will reflect the shape and mouth feel of caviar on the palate. A classic caviar accompaniment is crème fraîche and blinis. The acidity in champagne will cut through the creaminess like a warm knife through butter, and the toasty note of champagne will mimic the blini. This power pairing is, in every sense, a power couple, as each component is a luxury item in its own right!

German Riesling and Spicy Seafood Dishes

One of the best ways to counteract spice in a dish is with residual sugar (RS) in a wine. Choosing the right level of sweetness in certain German wines (e.g., Kabinett, Spätlese, and Auslese) and matching it with the heat in a spicy dish can lead to some wondrous pairings. German Riesling paired with mildly spicy seafood dishes is one such pairing. I personally love Riesling paired with Asian cuisine and sushi.

Sancerre and Goat's Cheese

One of the oldest adages in food and wine pairing reminds us, "If it grows together, it goes together." So, if you're ever stumped by what to pair with a dish, think of the regional origins of that dish and choose a wine that also comes from that region to complement it. It works wonderfully in this pairing of Sancerre and goat's cheese. Sancerre is 100 percent Sauvignon Blanc produced in France's Loire Valley. The Loire Valley is also famous for its great goat's milk cheeses. The delicate and aromatic nature of this wine complements the typically delicate, ashy texture and aromatic profile in goat's cheese. Also the high acidity helps break down the fattiness and creaminess of the cheese.

California Chardonnay and Pan-Roasted White Fish with Creamy Sauces

The full velvety texture of a mildly oaky California Chardonnay is a great companion to almost any delicately flavored white fish (halibut, turbot, ono/wahoo, etc.) served with butter-based sauces. The weight is identical, the viscosity of both the sauce and the wine will meld together, and the light oak will highlight the slight caramelization that is sure to be on the fish from the pan-roasting process. (Watch out for overly oaked Chardonnays that are always on restaurant wine lists. They are not food-friendly.)

Pinot Noir/Red Burgundy and Grilled Salmon

Because of the weight and high fat content of salmon, it requires a wine that is medium-bodied with a lot of acidity. Salmon also has a delicate sweet flavor that can easily be lost if paired with too overpowering a wine. Pinot Noir is an ideal mate here.

(continued)

(*continued*)

Bordeaux and Herb Crusted Lamb

Lamb is a very fatty red meat that requires a wine of judicious tannin and acidity to break down that fat. Since lamb also has a full body, it requires a wine that will match that body. Most Bordeaux (especially those of Pauillac, Saint-Julien, and Margaux) fit that bill perfectly. Often, Bordeaux show a slight lavender/rosemary aroma, which will complement the herb crust on the lamb as well.

Syrah/Shiraz and Braised Red Meats

Syrah is a reasonably high-alcohol wine with a medium-full to full body. It has medium tannin and acidity. This is perfect for braised beef. Don't forget, even though short ribs are a very fatty cut of beef, their fat has been mostly broken down already by the long, slow cooking method. The molasses-like viscosity of Syrah will seemingly melt in your mouth with the soft texture of the ribs.

How do you know if a particular food wine goes well with a particular food? A lot of it involves trial and error because not everyone's palate is the same. Indeed, people's palates are as unique as their fingerprints! Here's a simple rule of thumb, though. If you're thinking of pairing a certain wine with a certain food, do a side-by-side tasting comparison at home, before your event. Pour yourself a glass of the wine you want to serve, and at the same time, prepare the food item you want to pair with it. Now, dip your finger in the sauce or juice of the food item, touch your finger to your tongue, and as you do so, also take a sip of the wine. How does the mix of flavors taste? If you like what you taste, you have a winner. If not, you know that those two items are "flavor enemies" to quote my friends Andrew Dornenburg and Karen Page, authors of *Culinary Artistry* and other books. The items just don't pair up well together.

Although I want you to feel free to experiment and discover different pairings of wine and food that bring pleasure to *your* palate, there are some general rules of thumb as to what works best with what. Following are some general pointers about which wines to pair with which foods for an evening of fun and tasty merriment. Enjoy!

Beaujolais

Beaujolais is a wine with crisp acidity that allows it to cut through any fattiness of a dish. A good Beaujolais has bold, fruity qualities that allows it to be paired with fruit-dominant sauces as well as salty dishes where it works in contrast. For most people it is a highly drinkable wine because of its delightful sugar/acid balance, low tannins (tannic acid), and relatively low purchase price. Following are foods that work well with any kind of Beaujolais:

- Charcuterie (cold cuts)
- Pâtés (especially those with high fat content)
- Roasted chicken (coq au vin)
- Duck, game hen
- Cassoulet (a white bean stew that often contains pork, goose, or duck)
- Turkey (Thanksgiving)
- Pizza with fatty toppings
- Ham with fruity glaze

Bordeaux

Bordeaux is a complex, multilayered wine blended of five classic grapes (Cabernet Sauvignon, Cabernet Franc, Merlot, Malbec, and Petit Verdot). Its flavor is that of brambly black currant (cassis), licorice, black mushrooms, light hints of cedar, and pencil shavings—all of which are framed by a lovely, elegant texture. You can soften the firm tannins of a young Bordeaux (which give it a puckery taste) by combining them with grilled meats that have a high fat content. Here are some very good "dance partners" to pair with Bordeaux:

- Leg of lamb, rack of lamb, or herbed (rosemary) lamb chops
- Steaks of all kinds (especially well-marbled cuts like rib eye, porterhouse, and *entrecote*)
- Duck of all kinds (including *confit de canard*, which involves the leg of the duck)
- Roasted chicken (salty, garlic sauce)
- Goose

Burgundy—Red (Pinot Noir)

The comparatively cool climate of Burgundy, France, tends to create red burgundies (Pinot Noir) with a restrained elegance and a lovely acidity that works well in amplifying food flavors and cutting through rich sauces. Among the foods that go well with burgundy are:

- Grilled salmon (teriyaki) and other fatty fish
- Roasted chicken
- Pasta
- Casseroles
- Duck
- Game birds of all kinds
- Beef Bourguignon
- Roast pork with sausage
- Mushrooms of all styles
- Black truffles
- Bacon-inspired dishes

Burgundy—White

In my opinion, French white burgundy (Chardonnay) is one of the greatest food wines in the world. Because of the relatively chilly climate in which it is produced, French white burgundy possesses a steely acidity tinged with a flinty minerality. The wine acts just like a squeeze of lemon to cut through fattiness or rich sauces. Leaner white burgundies have citrusy notes and go well with:

- Roasted citrus chicken
- Shellfish (simply prepared)
- Delicate fish (simply prepared)

Fuller-bodied, richer styles of white burgundy work well with:

- Crab, lobster, shrimp, and scallops with buttery, cream sauces (*buerre blanc*)
- Seafood pasta casseroles
- Poached salmon (caper butter)
- Cedar planked salmon
- Sea bass
- Dover sole
- Veal a la crème

Cabernet Sauvignon

Cabernet Sauvignon expresses itself with notes of black currants, black cherries, blackberries, green or black olives, mint, and mushrooms. In young Cabernets, firm tannins (which create a puckery taste) go well with grilled meats that have a high fat content. In the mouth, this combination is magnetic! As Cabernets age and shed some of their tannic edge, more delicate meats should be considered to let the wine shine.

Cabernets (young and old) work well with all of the following:

- Full-flavored red meats
- Steaks (tri-tip, New York, rib eye, flank steak, etc.) with demi-glace sauces
- Lamb with rosemary, mustard, or your favorite herbs
- Prime rib
- Pork

- Veal chops
- Rabbit
- Barbecued ribs
- Grilled, smoked foods

Pinot Noir

Pinot Noir is one of my favorite red food wines. Characterized by notes of black cherries, strawberries, raspberries, cranberries, prunes, toasty spice, bacon fat, cola, and earthy mushrooms, the best Pinot Noirs come from France (Burgundy), Oregon, New Zealand, Italy, and California. Among food items to pair with Pinot Noir are:

- Duck
- Mushrooms of any sort
- Salmon (try teriyaki)
- Bacon
- Game birds
- Richly sauced pasta dishes
- Beef burgundy stews

Merlot

As a wine, Merlot expresses notes of blackberries, currants, black olives, plums, chocolate, red cherries, anise, cocoa, and bell peppers. Being generally softer in texture and tannins than some other reds, Merlots lend themselves to being paired with comfort foods of all types, including:

- Roasted lamb (herbs de Provence)
- Veal
- Burgers
- Meatloaf
- Flank steak

- Sausage
- Pizza
- Beef stews

Champagne and Sparkling Wines

You know that I love to start power entertaining events off with the service of champagne or sparkling wines. These can really set the tone for a dinner party or business reception. Foods that work well with champagne and sparkling wines include:

- Oysters/shellfish
- Smoked fish (trout, salmon)
- Snails
- Sushi/sashimi (any raw fish)—octopus!
- Tapas
- Quiches/omelettes (any egg dish)
- Caviar
- Fried foods (e.g., tempuras, calamari . . . hey, even onion rings!)

Chardonnay

Everyone is at least somewhat familiar with Chardonnay. Chardonnays exhibit notes of apple, lemon, pineapple, melon, vanilla, butterscotch, slightly burned toast, butter, figs, honey, and nuts. Most Chardonnays are medium- to full-bodied. Their weight thus lends them to use with bold flavors and rich sauces. Among my favorite foods to pair with Chardonnays are:

- Lobster, crab, scallops
- Oily white fish (monkfish, sea bass, halibut, salmon)
- Pasta with crème sauce
- Truffles

Chablis

Chablis, made from Chardonnay grapes, expresses itself with mineral-driven notes of flintiness and earthiness, as well as lively acidity. Use this as a stunt double for that slice of lemon to cut through rich sauces and amplify seafood specialties. Premier Cru and Grand Cru are full-bodied versions of Chablis and combine well with assertively flavored dishes, including:

- Oysters, shellfish
- Delicate white fish (Dover sole, gray sole, halibut cheeks)
- Grilled chicken
- Yellowtail (belly) sashimi
- Yellowtail collar (hamachi kama)

Power Pairing Wine and Food:
Advice from the Masters

As noted, powering pairing the right foods and wines is not a random thing. It takes experience and artistry, as well as imagination and audacity. I asked a few of my fellow Master Sommeliers to weigh in on how they design wine and food pairings, what they like to serve guests, and what they find makes people's palates water with anticipation.

My friend, Richard Dean, Master Sommelier at the Taj Campton Place in San Francisco, California, likes to pair butter-poached Maine lobster and crispy black rice, English peas, and mild coconut curry sauce with Riesling Kabinett Eitelsbacher Karthäuserhofberg Feinherb Mosel 2009. Why? "You get texture and flavor from the lobster and a mild heat from the curry that works very well with the sweetness and then the acidity from the wine," he says.

Jonathan Pullis, Master Sommelier and Wine Director at Montagna at the Little Nell Hotel in Aspen, Colorado, likes to marry the great lemon lime grapefruit crispness of Joel Gott Sauvignon Blanc with seasonal vegetables. "Seasonal vegetables and Sauvignon Blanc are always delicious together and healthy!" he exclaims.

Dustin Wilson, Master Sommelier and Wine Director at Eleven Madison Park in New York City, swoons over Southern Rhône Grenache with whole roasted duck. "It rocks," he says.

When I asked Brandon Tebbe, Master Sommelier and Director of Wine, Beverage and Restaurant at Paulée in Dundee, Oregon, he got playful and came up with several "favorite" power pairings. "My all-time favorite pairings are Riesling with cheese and charcuterie; a beautiful dry rosé on a patio with a Croque-Madame; spicy peppery Zinfandel and BBQ; Malbec or Syrah with a grilled steak; and bubbles with, well—pretty much anything!"

Roger Dagorn, Master Sommelier and Wine Director at Porter House New York, likes to pair one of his restaurant's daily specials, crispy soft-shell crabs, on a bed of ginger cucumber salad with a "floral, dry, unoaked Moschofilero from the house of Tselepos, Mantinia 2010."

Soft-shells are also a favorite of James Tidwell, Beverage Manager and Master Sommelier at the Four Seasons Resort and Club Dallas at Las Colinas, who notes that soft-shell crab over a bed of greens with a light citrus sauce "pairs with any champagne or dry sparkling wine."

Not everybody I spoke with offered up a favorite wine and food pairing. Andrea Robinson, Master Sommelier, author of *Great Wine Made Simple* and one of only a handful of female Master Sommeliers in the world, wanted to make the point that, in her view, matching wine and food isn't so much about the protein per se (red meat, fish, poultry, etc.) or the color of the wine (red or white) as it is about the food "prep." In other words, how you prepare a dish (grilled versus poached, for example) as well as what sauce, seasonings, and sides you include are what really should drive your choice of wine to go with that food. Preparation, she says, will "dictate the coolest pairing."

Other Factors in Designing
Wine and Food Pairings

Although selecting wine and food items that complement one another is the single biggest secret to effective power pairing, there are other factors to consider as well. Keep the guidelines noted here in mind to maximize people's enjoyment of the wine and food pairings you create:

👍 **Be certain that the weight of the wine matches the weight of the food dish.** As a yardstick here, think of the wine in terms of the weights of milk. For example:

- Light-bodied wines (like skim/nonfat milk)
- Medium-bodied wines (like 2 percent milk)
- Full-bodied wines (like whole milk)

👍 **Different foods call for different levels of acidity from a wine:**

- Higher-fat foods need more acidity to break down fat. So, for example, pair salmon with a high-acid Pinot Noir.
- Lower-fat foods go better with leaner wines. Thus, pair sole with white burgundies.

👍 **Match the flavors of the food with the flavors of the wine:**

- Pair earthy flavors with earthy wines. For example:

   Light mushrooms (oyster, crimini) and white burgundy
   Dark mushrooms (portabello, shiitake) and red burgundy

- Pair citrusy flavors with citrusy wines. For example:

   Grapefruit, lemon, lime, and Sancerre (Sauvignon Blanc)
   Oysters with lemon/cracked pepper and Chablis

- Pair sweet vegetable or fruit flavors with ripe wines. For example:

   Duck with fruit element and California/Oregon Pinot Noir
   White corn and California/Australian Chardonnay

- Pair foods with baking spice *(not heat spice)* with spicy wines. For example:

   Peppercorn-crusted steak with Zinfandel or cool climate Syrah

👍 **Opposites attract, so create pairings that contrast flavors (e.g., sweet/fruity versus salty):**

- Pair German Riesling with smoked salmon.
- Pair Port with Stilton cheese.

👍 **Balance spicy dishes with off dry to sweet table wines.**

- Pair Asian dishes with German Riesling (Kabinett, Spätlese).

👍 **Keep things in balance.** With simply prepared foods, use simple wines. You don't want the wine and food to fight each other during the pairing!

👍 **With older, more complex wines (\$\$\$), serve less intensely flavored foods so that the wine can grab center stage!**

👍 **If pairing a great red wine with meat, prepare the meat as simply as possible to ensure the focus is on the wine.**

👍 **When it comes to serving dessert wines, the higher the quality of the wine, the simpler the dessert should be.** Always be sure that the dessert is less sweet than the wine (think pound cake or unsugared shortbread cookies).

Resources for Power Pairing Wines and Foods

Before I conclude this chapter, let me recommend four books that go into the topic of pairing wines and foods in far more depth than I have in this chapter. First, my friend and fellow Master Sommelier Evan Goldstein has written two wonderful books that I heartily recommend: *Perfect Pairings* and *Daring Pairings*. Evan is a dynamic personality and a great speaker on the topics of food and wine. Both his books delve into the nuances of wine and food pairings with subtlety, creativity, and insight. Digest what each of them has to say, and you'll learn everything you ever need to know to design exciting wine and food pairings to serve at future power entertaining events.

Great Tastes Made Simple by Andrea Robinson is another must-have book for any power entertainer. Andrea, also a Master Sommelier, is one of the most renowned experts on the subject of food and wine on the planet today, a fact she proves in this book, in which she reveals some of the secrets of basic food tastes—sweet, earthy, savory, buttery, tart, and spicy—and how to pair these tastes with particular wines to maximize impact on people's palates.

Then there's *The Wine Bible* by Karen McNeal, which is an exhaustive "all about wine" book that deserves to be in everybody's wine book library. A leading wine educator, Karen is chairman of the Rudd Center of Wine Studies at the Culinary Institute of America in Napa Valley, California.

Finally, *The Food Lover's Guide to Wine* by Karen Page and Andrew Dornenburg is an indispensable reference guide that profiles 250 different wines by their essential characteristics—from body and intensity to distinguishing flavors along with ideal food pairings. I particularly enjoy their inclusion of insights from many of the best sommeliers in the United States.

Chapter Wrap-Up

This chapter has briefly outlined some of the great food and wine combinations you can incorporate into power entertaining events and that are sure to be crowd-pleasers when you do. It has also described some guidelines to follow in order to create balanced wine and food pairings.

Remember, power entertaining events can be designed for a few hundred people or a dozen; it's up to you. The bigger your event, the more likely it is that you'll want to enlist the help of a local wine merchant or professional sommelier to help you in planning the event and in designing appropriate and fun wine and food pairings for your get-together.

Power entertaining is easy if you plan ahead, manage your event well, and focus on giving your guests an enjoyable and memorable time. Now, let's move to Chapter 5 to talk about how you can enlist the help of wine professionals to help you plan your event and make it a success.

5

Your New Best Friends

The Sommelier and the Wine Merchant

P lanning and hosting power entertaining events takes careful thought and preparation. But don't think for a moment that you have to know everything there is to know about wine and food to put on a successful event. There's a whole army of wine professionals out there who can help you do this, and in this chapter, I introduce you to two of the most important partners you can enlist to help make your power entertaining events a success: sommeliers and wine merchants.

For anyone not familiar with the term, a sommelier (som-muhl-yeah) is a trained wine professional who often works in upscale restaurants, hotels, country clubs, wine bars, resorts, and even on cruise ships. They have deep knowledge and expertise in all areas of wine service and are typically involved in selecting, buying, stocking and storing wines, maintaining a restaurant's or resort's wine cellar, developing wine lists, and providing wine information and recommendations to restaurant patrons.

Typically a sommelier has a substantive knowledge not only of wine but also of beers, spirits, mixology, and food. They are frequently involved in training other restaurant staff about wine and wine service and are generally considered the in-house experts on all matters relating to alcoholic beverages.

Many sommeliers develop their knowledge of wine, and wine service, through years of formal academic study and practical coursework in winemaking and wine service. Typically, they also have extensive experience in the restaurant and hospitality industries. Becoming a credentialed sommelier takes a great deal of time and effort and can carry with it professional designations such as Master Sommelier (MS), Advanced Sommelier (AS), and Certified Sommelier (CS). Another professional designation one can earn is that of Master of Wine (MW). I'll have much more to say about sommelier education and professionalism in Chapter 10.

How a Sommelier Can Assist with Your Power Entertaining Events

In planning power entertaining events, I strongly recommend that you seek out and retain the services of a sommelier in your community. He or she can assist with all elements of event planning. This includes helping you:

- Become knowledgeable about entertaining with wine and food
- Determine and clarify your own wine preferences
- Design a wine and food menu for a power entertaining event
- Develop an event budget
- Create an event theme
- Identify specific wines, producers, and regions to feature
- Become acquainted with unusual or rare wines that may not generally be available or known to the public
- Purchase wines for the event
- Choose and secure a venue (e.g., restaurant) for an event
- Coordinate arrangements with caterers, restaurant, or hotel staff

They can also help by:

- Acting as "stage manager" of your event
- Serving as the on-site subject matter wine expert during your event

Where to Find a Sommelier

Finding potential sommeliers (aka somms) to work with you is relatively easy and can also be fun. Local upscale restaurants (what I call wine destination restaurants) and business-class hotels typically have sommeliers on staff. These folks will be only too happy to help you plan a business event that includes the service of food and wine. In addition, local cooking schools, gourmet food stores, and wine bars in your community can also put you in touch with local sommeliers whom you may want to contact and interview about their professional backgrounds and areas of expertise.

As a first step in finding a sommelier, do some online research. Visit the websites of some of the best restaurants in your area, as well as the websites of a few of the business-class hotels in your community. Review their menus and entertainment options; see if they have a sommelier on staff and if they have facilities to accommodate private parties, receptions, and dinners. Then, make arrangements to meet the somms at these places. Go prepared to talk with them about your potential needs and how you think they can be of assistance. You might even arrange to sample a few wines when you visit them! If you're new to all this, you may want to interview several sommeliers to get a sense of how they work and what they can do for you.

Preparing to Meet with a Sommelier

To get the most out of meetings or conversations with sommeliers, here are some questions to answer for yourself ahead of time:

- Do you have specific preferences or ideas about the service of wine at your event? Or are you open to different possibilities and looking for the sommelier to offer you a variety of wine/food tasting options and ideas?
- What are your favorite wines, and why do you like them? (For example, do you lean toward fruity wines or drier wines? Powerfully flavored wines or those that are more delicate in flavor?)
- What do you not like in wines (e.g., high acidity, tannic wines)?

- What specific services are you looking for the sommelier to perform for you?
  - Offer you wine suggestions.
  - Select and buy the wines for the event.
  - Suggest specific wine/food pairings.
  - Manage wine/food tastings at the event.
  - Coordinate with the kitchen/caterer, if necessary.
  - Offer guests background commentary and information about food/wines being served.
  - Serve as the on-site stage manager of the event.
- What's your budget for your event?
- Are you willing to pay a little more for something extra special?
- Who is the audience for the event? (For example, is it for businesspeople or family members? Sophisticated and knowledgeable wine drinkers and connoisseurs or not?)

A Passion for the Work

Talk to any really good sommeliers, and you'll quickly get a sense of how passionate they are about their work and how focused they are on creating enjoyable and memorable experiences for the guests who come to their restaurants.

At Addison, the signature restaurant of the Grand Del Mar near La Jolla, California, Wine Director Jesse Rodriguez presides over a 35,000-bottle wine cellar and sees himself as a "facilitator" of other people's enjoyment and pleasure when they walk in the door, be it for a business event or an intimate dinner with just one other person.

For Jesse, a major part of the sommelier role involves first sizing up people's desires and interests and their depth of wine knowledge. Then, he can determine how best to be of service to them, be it in suggesting a wine for a couple or foursome to share over dinner or in helping somebody plan a big corporate event. "We always want people to feel comfortable, never awkward," he says.

To help executives and banquet managers plan business dinners and client events, Jesse first asks people to give him their budget and to specify any wines they want to feature that night. After people answer these and other questions, he creates a detailed outline of wines and foods to serve at the event. The result, he says, often "blows clients away, especially when the menu makes the CEO (or other host of the event) look like a superstar" in the eyes of their guests.

And what if the executive or banquet manager doesn't know much about wine when contacting him for event planning advice? No problem, says Jesse. He and his wait staff are there to help. As the sommelier, Jesse offers suggestions about wine styles, regions, and foods to showcase (based on budget and the people attending) and works to build trust and rapport with the client in the process. He delights in putting clients at ease, likes to offer wine options that downplay widely promoted wine "scores," and sometimes encourages people to step beyond their comfort zone to try new things.

"In the end though, being a sommelier is all about building trust and rapport with people," says Jesse. It's a high-touch business that depends on one's credibility and empathy with others. You "have to connect with people where they are," he says. That's no problem for Jesse, who says he enjoys helping guests "be the stars of their events."

Not far from where Jesse works, another sommelier who's passionate about his work is Brian Donegan, Wine Director at Market Restaurant and Bar, a delightfully airy and upscale restaurant in Del Mar, California. Originally from New York City, where he learned just how important good food and wine can be in people's everyday lives, Brian works hard to make all guests of his restaurant feel welcome and to help them enjoy themselves when they walk in the door.

(*continued*)

(continued)

Market is a neighborhood restaurant and thus draws a crowd of regulars on many nights. The people who come to our restaurant "want to get away from their daily life and concerns for a couple of hours," he says. "They may have come for dinner with friends, or simply to hang out with the bartender or the sommelier or the chef, but in any case they're looking for an escape, the equivalent of a two- or three-hour vacation" away from their cares.

So what's Brian's philosophy of hospitality when it comes to the service of wine? "The first thing I do when I meet someone new is to ask them questions about their likes and dislikes. I might ask them what wines they've enjoyed in the past and also see if they want to check out something new." Once he gets to know a person's preferences and that person becomes a regular, he often finds himself becoming a personal wine consultant and coach to them. "I have a lot of guests who come in here and want me to pick wines for them," he says. "They say, 'Brian, it's amazing how well you know my palate!'" For Brian, this is a big part of why he delights in being a sommelier—the chance to get to know people well and advise them in a very personal way about wine.

What advice does Brian have for businesspeople on working with sommeliers? First, "be familiar with classical red wine varietals, like Cabernet, burgundy, and Sangiovese." Second, he says, get to know a good sommelier or wine merchant in your community and "leverage the knowledge" of that person to help you plan events and cultivate your palate (if you desire that). "Sommeliers and wine merchants have a lot of knowledge and are committed to serving others," says Brian, adding that "a good sommelier can help anyone grow in their knowledge and appreciation of wine."

He closed my interview with him for this book by noting that "people with a good palate and a curiosity about wine" will never be bored and will always have a wonderful and fascinating world to explore. I couldn't agree more!

Remember, sommeliers are wine professionals. They typically are very well informed about everything going on in the worlds of wine and food, and they can brief you on the latest trends in wine tasting and consumer preferences, the hottest new vintages, the up-and-coming wine producers and regions, the newest wine production techniques, and so on. Sommeliers often have access to rare and unusual wines that aren't generally on restaurant wine lists but that they hold in reserve for their best customers.

Many times, you'll get the most out of a sommelier by offering them a "small inducement" to bring the full range and depth of expertise to bear. This is where developing a little restaurant savvy and inside knowledge of the food and hospitality industry can really come in handy! (See Appendix C: "Don't Let the Restaurant *Happen* to You.")

I'll illustrate what I mean by telling you a story.

A few years ago I was invited to speak at an industry conference in Barcelona, Spain. While there, I was invited to dinner one night at one of Barcelona's finest restaurants. I wanted to make my group's evening out in Barcelona as spectacular as it could be. So, knowing where we'd be going for dinner that night, I got together with the sommelier at the restaurant about an hour or so before my group was to show up for dinner. I sat at the bar, found out who the sommelier was, and began to chat him up. We kibitzed a bit; I told him about my group and my interest in seeing to it that they got treated to something extra special that night when they came in. By the way, as I told the sommelier this, I dropped a few 20 euro notes in his hand and told him how much his efforts would mean to me.

Before long, my group arrived and asked for some Sparkling Cava (the toasting wine of choice in Spain) to start their evening off. At that point however, the sommelier jumped in to say that he and I had been talking and that, with their permission, he'd like to offer us something a little different to kick things off. This included Sercial Madeira and Manzanilla sherries with oysters. Well, I have to tell you, this took the evening to a whole new level and the rest of the evening proved just as spectacular (in part because I had offered the sommelier and waitstaff a generous tip upfront for their trouble!).

What Are 20- and 30-Somethings Drinking These Days?

To get a bead on what the younger generation is drinking (and thinking about wine) these days, I decided to ask a few questions of Christy Corcoran, a budding 20-something wine lover and wine writer based in the Boston area. She is currently studying to get her Certification as a Wine Specialist (CSW) from the Society of Wine Educators. Here are a few of the questions I asked her, and her answers:

Eddie: What kinds of wines are 20- and 30-somethings most interested in drinking today?

Christy: Generation X is looking for wines that are new and exciting, and a sense of place is very important! New world wines from places like Argentina, Chile, and the Pacific Northwest are popular because they feature some of the latest advancements in the craftsmanship of wine while maintaining the true flavors of their origins. Newer wineries also do a great job of marketing to young wine lovers. They often describe their wines in very clear and straightforward ways. Producers of increasingly popular blended wines, for example, will clearly state the wine's origin, list components, and include tasting notes when you buy bottles of these wines. This makes it easy for young consumers to make simple and easy choices of everyday inexpensive wines to purchase. Generic mass-produced wines are not the common choice of the X generation.

Eddie: What factors go into a young person's choice of a specific wine grower-producer today?

Christy: My generation makes choices every day, from the food we eat to the cars we drive, based on our concern for the environment and our precious dwindling natural resources. This extends to our choices of wine. Wine can be produced organically, biodynamically, or sustainably. All factors considered, I think sustainable viticulture is the most consistent and accessible way for modern eco-friendly oenophiles to indulge in wine with a clear conscience. Sustainable vineyards treat their slice of earth with the tender loving care that will preserve their soil's richness for generations to come. This tenderness translates to the taste and personality of the wines these vineyards produce.

Eddie: What do you personally look for in a wine?

Christy: Terroir! (a sense of the place where the wine was produced; its geographical pedigree) Wines that are deeply connected to their growing site stimulate my interest to want to travel to that location and see the vineyard for myself!

Eddie: What do you see as your role as a wine educator and expert?

Christy: As a wine professional, my role isn't to judge an individual's taste preferences but only to help people decipher and fully appreciate what they are tasting.

Eddie: Can you describe your philosophy of hospitality and the role wine plays in that?

Christy: Good wine (and food) have been bringing people together for centuries. Throughout history, all social classes and cultures have used it, both for celebrations and everyday bonding. Whether it is the sharing of a special bottle for high holidays or the use of wine as a consistent bonding element over a family dinner, wine is implicitly human. All that said, wine is only as good as the company with which it is shared!

This story illustrates an approach that you yourself may want to take in dealing with sommeliers and other restaurant staff as well, especially if you want to take power entertaining events to a special level. When you engage a sommelier to help you plan an event, always be prepared to offer a financial inducement upfront. This will help ensure that you get the extra measure of quality and service you want from that individual. Even in the case of an initial meeting with a sommelier, you can employ this strategy. Meet at the sommelier's restaurant, sit at the bar, and get to know them a bit and give that person a chance to get to know you. As you do this, check to see that the chemistry between the two of you is good and that the ambience and style of the restaurant are right for your event.

Offer the sommelier a couple of $20 bills during your initial conversation (to indicate you're serious). Ask the sommelier if they have "anything special" that can be served at your reception or dinner, things not on the menu or wine list but that they think would appeal to your guests and "kick things up a notch." The sommelier will get where you're coming from and what you're asking for, believe me! Ask all the questions I list in this chapter; then ask the sommelier to prepare a sample wine and food menu for your review. On leaving, tell the sommelier how much you appreciate their efforts on your behalf.

If, for some reason, you don't have the luxury of stopping in to meet with the sommelier in person ahead of time (perhaps you live in another city), you can still look over the restaurant's online wine list, find out who the sommelier is, and have a meaningful conversation with that person over the phone and communicate your wishes. Tell the sommelier that if things go well, you'll offer them and the waitstaff a 25 percent tip on the final bill. (Yes, I know it seems hefty, but it can really help take wine and food service at your event to a whole new level.)

Remember, sommeliers are there to help you create an experience for your guests . . . one that is enjoyable, meaningful, and educational. This is their art and trade. Take care of them on the front end and they'll take care of you for an entire evening.

Introducing the Wine Merchant

As part of planning and hosting power entertaining events, another wine professional you want to get to know is the wine merchant. Often a retailer who owns one or more wine stores or shops, this is a person who knows food and wine well, who might have been a sommelier in the past, and who also entertains. The wine merchant should be able to work closely with you and/or your sommelier to help plan your event and secure wines and vintages that others may not be able to procure.

Where to Find a Wine Merchant

A good wine merchant can be hard to find. You don't want to work just with a liquor store owner or "bottle shop" operator. You want the real deal, so you may want to find people through referral. Again, talk to the owners of local gourmet food shops, to the people who run local culinary arts programs in your community, or even to your friendly liquor store owner who might know somebody appropriate with whom you can work. Once you find the right person, talk to them about your goals and objectives for your event and meet to discuss possible wines to feature. Many wine merchants produce monthly newsletters through which they keep their clients informed about the latest news and developments in the worlds of wine and food. Many also have wine bars, wine dispensers, and/or tasting rooms on their premises where you can sample wines that they suggest to you.

Coming Up with Potential Themes for Your Event

Discuss potential themes for your event with the wine merchant, and bring with you some of the suggested pairings of wine and food that I outline in Chapters 4 and 6. This will give the wine merchant possibilities to consider.

Possible themes for your power entertaining event could include any of the following (and many others):

- Getting to know the various kinds of Chablis
- Did you know that Beaujolais means more than Beaujolais Nouveau?
- Getting to know the three Bs of Italy—Barolo, Barbera, and Barbaresco
- Wines of the Pacific Northwest

- California versus Oregon Pinot Noirs
- Dry German food wines
- Understanding the wine regions of Spain
- Old World versus New World Cabernets

A Wine Merchant with a Mission

Damon Goldstein, co-owner (with his wife Sabrina) of Truly Fine Wines in San Diego, California, is a wine merchant on a personal mission: to bring the joys of German wines to the American wine drinking public, which he feels doesn't appreciate either the nuances or varieties of wines that are produced in Deutschland.

"Most people associate Germany with Rieslings, and sweet, cheap Rieslings in small blue bottles at that," says Damon. But, he adds, the country also produces wonderful dry Rieslings, Pinot Noirs, sparking wines, and indigenous varietals. For this reason, Damon decided some years ago to focus on popularizing German wines and educating Americans about them. Today, Damon and Sabrina maintain a diversified grower-producer portfolio of dry German wines that they feature both in their store and also online at: www.trulyfinewine.com. "We want to offer people a versatile portfolio that reflects what good-quality producers are doing in Germany," Damon says.

Damon says his affection for German wines began when he and Sabrina started dating back in the late 1990s. He would travel to Germany to spend time with his future German-born wife, and, as he tells it, "We drank some extraordinary wines together on the banks of the Rhine where people have been enjoying good wine for thousands of years."

Soon enough, Goldstein was as head over heels for German varietals as he was for Sabrina, and his mission to bring word of German wines to Americans took root.

As for educating Americans about Riesling, Damon says he wants Americans to know that Riesling isn't always sweet.

In fact, it can be very dry and is perhaps the most versatile white varietal available in the world today. That's one reason it's so popular among sommeliers, and a surefire dance partner with a wide variety of foods. "You can pair Riesling with almost any meal, including meals that feature red meat," says Damon. This is because of its great balance of acid and sugar, a harmony that reflects the dedication and artisanship of German wine producers.

Indeed, Damon is so impressed with the skill of German winemakers that he likens them to that country's automakers. Like German automakers, he says, Germany's wine producers bring an "engineered, laser-like quality approach to wine production that you can taste in every bottle of German wine."

Questions the Wine Merchant Will Ask *You*

Like the sommelier, the wine merchant has an in-depth knowledge of food and wine and can work with you and/or the sommelier to design a menu and event to your liking. Wine merchants have their own professional contact and procurement networks and can buy wines at rates that others may not be able to offer. They can also recommend specific vintages, producers, and regions from which to buy wine for your event. All of this would take you months, if not years, to determine for yourself. Good wine merchants will be attentive to your needs. And although they want your business, they won't simply try to push wines on you to generate revenue for themselves. They will, instead, ask you questions such as the following:

- What kind of event are you planning? Is it a business event, a family gathering, a wedding, a client appreciation event, a special celebration for you and your spouse, a child's graduation from college, or something else?
- What's your budget?
- What kinds of wine do you like? What kinds do you not like?

- What do you want to accomplish through your event?
- Would you like me to look around for wines that may appeal to you so that you can sample them ahead of your event?

Sampling Wines on Your Own

As noted, some wine merchants have special wine dispensers on their premises through which you can sample small portions of different varieties of wine. In some cases, you will also find these self-service wine dispensers in hotels, bars, and restaurants, and if you do, I suggest you check them out.

One leading manufacturer of such dispensers is an Italian company called Enomatic Wine Serving Systems (www.enomaticusa. com). This company, based in Tuscany, has pioneered the service of different kinds of wine in restaurant, resort, and wine bar settings. It allows patrons to sample just small amounts of wine to compare and contrast different wine varieties that would be expensive to buy as full glasses (much less as entire bottles)! Enomatic's wine dispensers enable you to put a credit card into the machine, and then, for a set amount—say, $100—you can sample a variety of wines that you probably wouldn't be inclined to buy as a full bottle (or even a glass) because of their price.

Not long ago, I visited a casino in Reno, Nevada, that had one of these self-serve dispensers on site. I have to say these devices are addictive! I dropped more money into one of them that night than I did into any of the casino's slot machines! It's very easy to do because you can buy just a single ounce of a rare wine that might cost $100 a bottle or more. It doesn't take long to spend the $100 you've had debited from your credit card for this purpose, especially when a single ounce serving costs $20-plus! Some restaurants, wine bars, and hotels have several dispensers on their premises and offer a variety of wines ranging in price from $20 to $60 a bottle. They'll also have exclusive VIP rooms with additional machines that feature extremely rare and expensive wines for prices you can only imagine. If interested, here's the website to the Reno casino I visited where there are self-service Enomatic wine bars on site. If you go there, have fun but guard your wallet!

www.grandsierraresort.com/bars-lounges/other-bars-lounges/
the-reserve

If you happen to travel a lot on business, or find yourself in a big resort city, such as Las Vegas, New Orleans, or elsewhere, do a Web search to see what hotels or casinos in that city have self-service wine bars on the premises. You'll probably have a lot of fun sampling some really wonderful wines. And who knows? You might even taste a few that you'll want to feature at future power entertaining events!

Finding Wines Online

Although working with a sommelier or wine merchant is the ideal way to locate and buy wines for power entertaining events, there may be times when you simply can't find a sommelier or wine merchant in your local community. In that case, you can easily turn to the Internet for resources. In directing you to Web-based wine merchants, however, let me first say something about how I classify wines.

I divide wines into three general categories, and depending on the audience and occasion, I will purchase wines online from one category or another for the power entertaining events I host. The categories of classification I use are as follows:

👍 *Beverage Wines:* These are common everyday wines. Cost: Up to $12 a bottle.

👍 👍 *Better Wines:* These are wines for weekends and special occasions with good friends. They are a notch up in quality from beverage wines and have a certain fruitiness that gives them a unique personality. Cost: Up to $50 bottle.

👍 👍 👍 *Best Wines:* These are wines that take your breath away and that you'll want to serve to your foodie friends who recognize excellence. Cost: Generally $50 and up.

You can easily find *beverage* wines at the large chain liquor stores, so there's no need to buy these online. If you're fortunate to have a Trader Joe's in your area, you're lucky, as they carry beverage wines as well. Trader Joe's buyers are very skilled and their wine selection reflects both great variety and great value.

Generally, *better* wines can be found at your favorite wine shops and also at Costco, which has the best prices of any wine retailer. *Costco is cool!* It's also the largest wine retailer in the United States.

Finding the *best (premium) wines* is a challenge. In some cases, the distribution of these wines is tightly allocated, making them scarce commodities. In other cases, premium wines that win critical acclaim from wine and food critics, or that are designated as "collector's items," often vanish quickly from the marketplace once any news appears about them in the wine and food press. Because of these realities you need to act fast to buy premium wines whenever you taste or hear of a great premium wine.

Note: For more on the different categories of wine and what to consider in planning power entertaining events, see Appendix B.

Wine Websites to Know and Trust

One of the very best places to shop for premium wines is online, which is where I do a lot of my wine shopping. One of my favorite wine websites is www.wine-searcher.com. On this site, you simply type in the name of the wine and vintage you're looking for, and the site immediately directs you to liquor stores and wine merchants all over the country where you can purchase it. The service is free, but I suggest you invest $29.00 for the pro version of the service, which gives you a better wine selection from around the country (and the world). Being a subscriber to wine-searcher.com is essential if you want to acquire wines that will dazzle your guests. On this site you'll also get great value for the wines you buy.

More than 80 percent of my cellared wines are from Bordeaux, Burgundy, Italy, and Germany, and besides using www.wine-searcher .com I also use the following sites to find and buy wines I like:

- *The Burgundy Wine Company:* www.burgundywinecompany .com. Located in New York City, this store has an incredible wine selection from Burgundy, Oregon, and the Rhône Valley. If you get to the Big Apple, you should check them out in person. They're located in downtown Manhattan. At the very least, get on their e-mail list.

- *Kermit Lynch Wine Merchant:* www.kermitlynch.com. This is one of my favorite wine merchants. What's fabulous about this store is that Kermit sources obscure and unique Old World wines that range in price from $10 to $30 per bottle (and up). In my experience, Kermit wines are often unique and offer very good value for the money. Get on Kermit's monthly catalog list and you'll continually hear about wines that will impress and dazzle your guests.

- *Truly Fine Wine:* www.trulyfinewine.com. I love this site because for me it is the "go to" place to get dry style "halbtrocken" and "trocken" German Riesling. Truly Fine Wine is a new company that has some of the finest selections of these wines at extremely reasonable prices. Check out the Truly Fine Wine website and order a sampler pack from Damon.

Here are still other great online wine merchants to check out:

- Jeffrey M. Davies Signature Selections: Contact Jeffrey directly at jmdavies@signature-selections.com
- Wine Exchange: www.winex.com
- The Wine Club: www.thewineclub.com
- K&L Wines: www.klwines.com
- Bounty Hunter Rare Wine and Provisions: www.bountyhunter wine.com
- Premier Cru: www.premiercru.com
- Appellation America: www.appellationamerica.com
- NapaCabs.com: wine-club-central.com
- Wines Til Sold Out: www.wtso.com
- Twenty Twenty Wine Merchants: www.2020wines.com
- Garagiste: www.garagistewine.com
- Brown Derby International Wine Center: www.brownderby .com
- Avalon Wine: www.avalonwine.com

When buying wines online, always buy wines "in pairs" for purposes of side-by-side comparisons. Obviously, you'll want to buy as many pairs as may be needed to include the pairing as part of a power entertaining event. So buy (and budget) accordingly. Again, you may want to refer to Chapter 6 for wine pairings to try.

Need the services of a sommelier to help you plan your next business event? Visit my website: www.eddieosterland.com to get information on nearly 5,000 sommeliers across the United States who may be able to assist you.

Chapter Wrap-Up

Planning a power entertaining event, reception, or dinner takes careful thought, planning, and preparation but thankfully you don't have to do it alone. As I've discussed in this chapter, both sommeliers and wine merchants are great resources to tap to help you plan these events and manage them successfully each and every time. There are also many excellent online wine merchants and wine sites where you can buy wines, learn about the hottest new vintages and producers, and do much, much more.

Let's go on now to Chapter 6, where I talk in detail about sampling wines in dynamic pairs. After reading Chapter 6, you'll no doubt have ideas and preferences about the kinds of wine you'd like to serve at power entertaining receptions and dinners and will be able to take that information to both sommeliers and wine merchants for further discussion and event planning.

6

So Many Wines, So Little Time!

All you need to know to distinguish yourself as a power entertainer!
—Eddie O.

To prepare for conversations with wine merchants and somme- liers, it's important to have a good working knowledge of wine so that you know what questions to ask and what kinds of wine to potentially serve at power entertaining functions. For that reason, in the pages that follow, I offer thumbnail descriptions of important wine regions and describe unique pairings of wine that will both sur- prise and delight guests at power entertaining events. Pick and choose among these pairings when planning power entertaining functions, and I guarantee you that people will want to attend your social events time and time again!

The wines we will discuss in this chapter include:

- Beaujolais
- Bordeaux (Left Bank and Right Bank)

- Burgundy (Red and White)
- Pinot Noir
- Sparkling wines
- Wines of the Pacific Northwest
- Cabernet Sauvignon
- Merlot
- California wines
- German wines
- Chablis
- Italian wines
- Spanish wines
- Rhône wines
- Chilean, Argentinean, and South African wines
- Other wines
- Fortified wines
- Port (Portugal)
- Premium sake
- Beer

Beaujolais

Beaujolais has a reputation of being the "fun" red wine on many people's preferred drinking lists. Produced from the Gamay grape in the Beaujolais province of France, it's very fruity but also low in tannins and high in acidity, qualities that make it a very drinkable wine to many people, especially when it's served slightly chilled. Because of its vibrant acidity, Beaujolais is easily paired with food. Best of all, most Beaujolais is inexpensive and thus a perfect party wine!

There are four categories of Beaujolais wines. They are shown in descending order of quality in Figure 6.1.

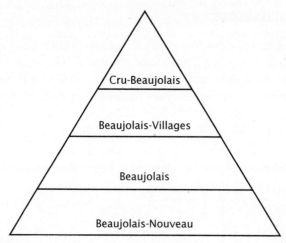

FIGURE 6.1   The Four Types of Beaujolais

Cru Beaujolais

Cru (meaning "growth") is a French wine term that denotes a wine of high quality or from a region where wine is produced. Cru Beaujolais is the highest-quality Beaujolais one can buy. It comes from just 10 of the more than 96 different villages within the Beaujolais region of France where Beaujolais is produced. The 10 highest-quality Cru Beaujolais include Brouilly, Côte de Brouilly, Morgon, Chénas, Chiroubles, Fleurie, Juliénas, Moulin-à-Vent, Régnié, and Saint-Amour.

Beaujolais—Villages

These Beaujolais wines are of intermediate quality and are produced in 1 of 39 specific villages in the Haut Beaujolais region of France.

Beaujolais

This designation refers to Beaujolais wines produced in any of 60 French villages in the northern part of the Beaujolais wine region.

Beaujolais Nouveau

This designation is given to young Beaujolais wine that is most often drunk as "jug wine" in France and elsewhere. The grapes for this variety of Beaujolais are harvested between late August and early September each year, and they are released to the public on the third Thursday of November—Beaujolais Nouveau Day. It is the first French wine to be released for each vintage year.

👍 Pairing #1: Cru Morgon versus Cru Moulin-à-Vent

In this first pairing I challenge you to distinguish between two very different styles of Cru Beaujolais: Morgon and Moulin-à-Vent. You'll find that the Morgon has an unmistakably soft texture, haunting finish, and an aroma that can range from cranberries to boysenberries. It often displays a Burgundian character of silky texture. By contrast, the Moulin-à-Vent is more sturdily structured, has higher tannins, and is a bit more "masculine." In other words, it is fuller bodied. Some producers age their Moulin-à-Vent in oak, which gives it still more tannin and structure. The phrase *fûts de chêne* (oak casks) sometimes appears on the wine labels of these oak-aged wines.

Which of these Crus do you prefer? Consult your wine merchant or sommelier to pair up different combinations of the 10 Cru Beaujolais that exist. You'll have a blast!

Bordeaux (Left Bank and Right Bank)

A Bordeaux wine (red or white) can be defined as any wine produced in the Bordeaux region of France. This region of France has been cultivating vines for more than 2,000 years and has perhaps the highest reputation for fine wines in the entire world.

The Bordeaux vineyard appellation is one of the largest in France. Although the region is best known for its reds, a variety of both whites and reds are produced in Bordeaux. Unlike other regions in France, where wines are made from single grape varieties, Bordeaux blends five major grape varieties into the production of its reds. These include Cabernet Sauvignon, Merlot, Cabernet Franc, Malbec, and Petit Verdot. White Bordeaux wines are also typically blends, usually of Sémillon and Sauvignon Blanc. Bordeaux reds are elegantly styled, with firm tannin levels that develop a characteristic softness and subtlety with age. Their age worthiness makes them ideal wines for collecting and cellaring.

There are two major growing areas in Bordeaux: the Left Bank and the Right Bank. These names are derived from the location of each area to the left (west) or right (east) of the Gironde River. The Left Bank consists of seven subregions, each with its own *AOC*, or *Appellation d'Origine Contrôlée/Protégée (AOC/AOP)*, the term that the European Union uses to define products of distinct regional origin. These are spread across two subdivisions: Médoc and Graves. The Right Bank, located near the city of Libourne, consists of two subdivisions: Saint-Émilion and Pomerol. Each of Bordeaux's various subregions displays unique characteristics of its *terroir*, that is, its soil, climate, weather, drainage, and so forth.

The four levels of quality of Bordeaux wines, in the ascending order of quality, are shown in Figure 6.2.

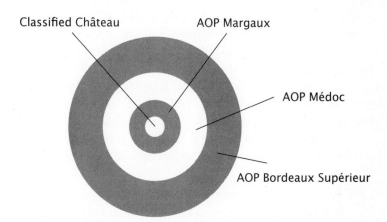

FIGURE 6.2 The Four Types of Bordeaux

AOP Bordeaux Supérieur

In the outer circle of the diagram shown in Figure 6.2, you will find regional (AOP Bordeaux Supérieur) wines. Wines with this regional appellation are the least expensive wines of the Bordeaux family and are typically described as "ready-to-drink" wines.

Subregional and Village Bordeaux

As you move closer to the center, you experience more concentrated wines from specific subregions like Médoc and Graves, as well as villages like Margaux, Saint-Julien, Pauillac, and Saint-Estèphe. Wines from villages like Margaux or Saint-Estèphe are more expensive and more concentrated in flavor than their Bordeaux Supérieur cousins.

Classified Châteaux

At the center of the circle are wines with specific personalities that come from single vineyard estates known as châteaux. In 1855, Bordeaux was the first wine region in the world to officially classify high-performing estates, or châteaux. They were delineated into five layers of Crus (or growths), and it is these Crus that represent the highest quality of Bordeaux today. Châteaux-bottled wines are meant to age for three to five years, but wines from the most expensive and famous properties are capable of lasting 30 years in good vintages. Since the original classification system was put in place in 1855, many additional estates have achieved similar levels of wine quality but also represent some of the best values in Bordeaux available today. Ask your somm or wine merchant to tell you about these.

Here are two paired Bordeaux tastings I recommend. Ask your local sommelier or wine merchant to recommend specific producers.

👍 Pairing #2: Margaux versus Saint-Estèphe (Left Bank Bordeaux)

This wine pairing offers a classic matchup between finesse on the one hand (Margaux) and raw power (Saint-Estèphe) on the other. Margaux produces elegant wines that create a silky feel in your mouth. They are often ready to drink earlier than wines from other famous communes of the Left Bank. Saint-Estèphe, on the other hand, the Haut-Médoc's northernmost commune, produces big, full-bodied, firm tannic wines, which are slow to mature. You'll note in this pairing that the Margaux is rather feminine (silky and restrained) in style; the Saint-Estèphe, more masculine. Which do you like better? Keep in mind that these wines are of equal quality, so the differences really boil down to stylistic distinctions between the two. What stylistic distinctions can you make in sampling both?

👍 Pairing #3: Cru Artisan versus Classified Châteaux (Left Bank Bordeaux)

Both wines in this pairing are at the level where Bordeaux gets really serious. As noted, in the nineteenth century the Bordelaise were the first to identify estates that produced the best-quality wines and classify them into tiers. This became the basis of the Cru system, still used today. Today there are 61 officially recognized Classified Châteaux in Bordeaux. Two additional designations to be aware of are Cru Artisan and Cru Bourgeois. Cru Artisan wines currently represent 44 small producers throughout the Médoc. This designation indicates wines made in adherence to strict quality standards. Cru Bourgeois, seen on older bottles, used to identify wines of similar quality to that of Cru Artisan. However, this term is no longer used as a specific classification.

As you sample the Cru Artisan, notice that its flavors are very focused and layers of complexity begin to surface as you hold it in your mouth for a few seconds. Cru Artisan wines are lovely, yet they are reasonably priced, compared with Classified Châteaux wines. Think of Cru Artisan as an "upper middle class" Bordeaux.

In contrast to Cru Artisan wines, Classified Châteaux wines are produced by 1 of just 61 classified properties of the Left Bank, representing the best wines of Bordeaux. The nuances of flavor in these wines defy easy description in words, and great vintages of these pedigree wines command stratospheric prices because they're considered the royalty of the region.

👍 Pairing #4: Saint-Émilion versus Pomerol (Right Bank Bordeaux)

In this pairing, sample two wines that embody the stylistic differences between the communes of Saint-Émilion and Pomerol. These are the two appellations that most collectors think of when somebody mentions the Right Bank. Saint-Émilion is a must-see medieval town 22 miles northeast of Bordeaux. The majority of wines produced there are red and contain a high percentage of Merlot (60 percent of the blend), as well as Cabernet Franc (around 30 percent) and Cabernet Sauvignon (roughly 10 percent). Because of the high percentage of Merlot in them, Saint-Émilion wines are more "approachable" than wines from the Left Bank. The best are full-bodied and fleshy, making them ideal restaurant wines.

Pomerol is located northwest of Saint-Émilion and also produces wines made predominantly of Merlot (oftentimes close to 100 percent), with some Cabernet Franc blended in for structure and added complexity. The best Pomerol wines are ripe, plummy, and richly flavored.

Which of these wines you prefer is mostly a matter of personal preference. What's important to note here is that both wines are generally more ready to drink than those from the Médoc (Left Bank) and should be in the cellars of any serious wine enthusiast.

Burgundy (Red and White)

If Bordeaux is sometimes called the king of wines, then burgundy is often thought of as the queen. Some of the greatest and most memorable wine experiences any wine lover has ever had can be traced back to the vineyards and wine cellars of France's Burgundy wine region. But unfortunately, there are a few horror stories (or at least wines we'd like to forget) that have emerged out of this region as well. That's because many factors (soil content, drainage, slopes, and angle to the sun, among many others) can all affect the concentration, flavor profiles, and quality of the wines produced in this region. These variables are collectively referred to as *terroir*. Terroir is an extremely important concept in understanding the texture, configuration, and flavor of burgundy.

The finest vineyard sites in Burgundy face the sun. Having sufficient sunlight is critical to the ripening of grapes, and when it comes to cultivating Burgundy grapes, this is sometimes problematic. Burgundy is a very cool growing region, and in years when sunlight isn't abundant, highly acidic and thin wines are often the result.

When it comes to grape varieties produced in Burgundy, it's quite simple: red burgundies are almost exclusively made from Pinot Noir grapes; the white burgundies, from Chardonnay grapes.

Types of Burgundy

There are four quality levels of burgundy to be aware of. I've listed these in ascending order of quality and price in Figure 6.3.

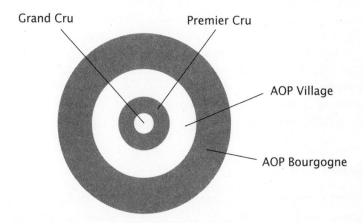

FIGURE 6.3   The Four Types of Burgundy

Generic (AOP Bourgogne)

This is the regional level of wine production in Burgundy and the level at which there are the fewest restrictions on wine production. When balanced, generic burgundies can be good, everyday values to buy. On their labels you will see *Appellation Bourgogne Contrôlée*, which is the most general AOP *(Appellation d'Origine Protégée)* in Burgundy.

AOP Village

These burgundies offer better quality with more focused flavors. (Notice the more specific appellation.) They represent the majority of wines produced in Burgundy (36 percent of production). Examples include *Appellation Côte de Beaune-Villages* and *Côte de Nuits-Village*, where wines from several villages are blended into a regional style. A slightly higher quality level would be reflected in a single village name such as *Appellation Volnay Contrôlée* or *Appellation Pommard Protégée*.

Premier Cru

Burgundies at this level are from a specific vineyard listed on the label. They have more stringent restrictions placed on their production (such as yield restrictions of 45 hectoliter/hectare) and represent just 12 percent of total annual burgundy production. An example of a Premier Cru label is *Appellation Volnay Premier Cru-Clos des Chênes* (vineyard). These wines should have a higher quality level than those with just a village name. Most will benefit from three to five years of aging. As they mature, they begin to get expensive, so buy these wines when they're young and hold them in reserve for later.

Grand Cru

Grand Crus are exclusive burgundies selected from the 32 Grand Cru vineyard sites in Burgundy. These are the wines that have made Burgundy famous. They are seductive, rare, and very expensive. They represent just 2 percent of Burgundy's annual wine production, with even more stringent production standards in place than for Premier Crus (35 hectoliter/hectare). Unfortunately, the integrity of producers, or *domains*, varies greatly, so wines in this category must be selected carefully. Grand Crus are wines for cellaring and need five to seven years before they reach their peak of flavor. The greatest examples will mature for 30-plus years. Great Grand Cru burgundy is something every wine lover needs to experience in their lifetime!

Two suggested pairings of red burgundy follow.

👍 Pairing #5: Côte de Beaune versus Côte de Nuits

In this pairing I introduce you to burgundies made in two of France's outstanding wine-producing regions: the Côte de Beaune in the south of Burgundy and the Côte de Nuits in the north. Pinot Noirs produced in the warmer Côte de Beaune area tend to be softer in texture than those from Côte de Nuits. The warmer weather means the grapes ripen and get harvested earlier, and they avoid some of the late rains that can plague the vineyards of Côte de Nuits. That said, the shorter time on vine means that Côte de Beaune grapes miss developing the characteristics of added complexity, layers of flavors, and tannin that typify Côte de Nuits wines.

In my view the best Pinot Noirs in the world are grown in the Côte de Nuits, where the grapes enjoy added "hang time" on the vine. The texture of these wines is richer and the flavors deeper and more intense with firm tannins.

👍 Pairing #6: Village versus Premiere Cru

In this pairing, select a village-level burgundy from the Côte de Nuits to pit against a Premier Cru. The quality of the village-level burgundy is good, as you know. But in this pairing the Premier Cru should be the superior wine. Drink these fine burgundies, and you'll soon discover that great burgundy has wonderful texture; in fact, it's like drinking satin. It's both rich and soft, whether light, medium, or full-bodied. Great burgundies also display a fine balance of fruit, acidity, tannin, and earthiness. If just one of these qualities overshadows the others, the wine can seem one-dimensional.

Following is a suggested paired tasting of white burgundy.

👍 Pairing #7: Meursault versus Puligny-Montrachet

These two top-quality wines are easily two of the most famous in the Côte de Beaune (if not all of Burgundy). However, their styles could not be more different. The deft elegance of Meursault makes it one of the most recognizable wines of Burgundy. What makes it so notable is the juxtaposition of sensory sensations you experience in first sniffing and then tasting it. Meursault's greatness lies in the difference between its nose (aroma) and its taste. Great Meursault smells creamy and toasty with a note of hazelnut. But, when you taste it, it is mineral-driven to its core! This dichotomy is the hallmark of Meursault. It's a wine with a wonderful split personality.

By comparison with Meursault, Puligny is the closest example that France makes to a big, buttery California Chardonnay. It is, in fact, the most powerful AOP for Chardonnay in the Côte de Beaune. That said, this French version of Chardonnay is very different from its California cousin and the Meursault. While Meursault is elegant, Puligny is powerful! See how much so in your side-by-side comparison of these two white burgundies.

Pinot Noir

Pinot Noir is one of the greatest grape varietals. Moderately high in acid, it is the foundation of some of the most sought after and expensive wines in the world, in part because of its extraordinary versatility matched only by Riesling. Pinot Noir's body can range from light to medium; its tannin levels, from low to medium; and its alcohol level, from medium to medium high. Pinot Noir can have aromas of fruits, specifically red cherries, cranberries, raspberries, strawberries, and rhubarb. It can also smell of nonfruits, including flowers, cola, pine needles, and bacon fat. Finally, it can have an earthy nose suggestive of mushrooms, truffles, wet hay, and even the forest floor.

Pinot Noir is produced in a number of classic regions, including:

- France: Burgundy (the ground zero of Pinot Noir production), the Loire Valley (Sancerre Rouge), and Champagne
- Germany (where it's called Spätburgunder or Late Burgundian for its late ripening characteristic)

It's also made in:

- California: Santa Barbara, Monterey, Sonoma, Carneros, Anderson Valley
- Oregon: Willamette Valley, Willamette sub AVAs (Chehalem Mountains, Eola-Amity Hills, Ribbon Ridge, and others)
- New Zealand: Central Otago, Marlborough, Martinborough, Gisborne
- Italy: Piedmont, Lombardy, Alto Adige
- Australia: Yarra Valley, Mornington Peninsula, Geelong

Pinot Noir grapes love a cool climate and soil rich in clay and volcanic ash. That said, they are finicky grapes that require warm (not hot) days to ripen and cool nights to retain their acidity. They also require a long time to ripen properly on the vine and a lot of care and attention along the way. (This is one reason Pinot Noir can be either very good or quite forgettable.) When Pinot Noir grapes ripen well, the results are extraordinary. That's because when harvested, they can reflect their terroir like almost no other grape, a quality that shines through in the very best Pinot Noirs sold today.

👍 **Pairing #8: French Burgundy versus California Pinot Noir**
Here's a Pinot Noir pairing you'll enjoy. It pits a classic French burgundy against a California (New World) Pinot Noir. French burgundy is considered the Holy Grail of Pinot Noir for winemakers around the world. But today the best producers of the New World are striving to capture some of the richness and character of classic French burgundy in the Pinot Noirs produced in the United States and elsewhere. So what do you experience as you taste these two wines side by side? What stylistic or character differences do you discern?

Hint: For this pairing, ask your wine merchant to choose a benchmark burgundy that is complex, earthy, and smoky with bright acids and voluptuous texture. The Burgundians have been growing the same grapes in the same places for so many generations that they know exactly which wines perform best in which areas. As with other wines, they have developed a Cru system of quality designation. In Burgundy's case, this includes four levels of quality, including:

- Level 1: Simple regional burgundy (Bourgogne)
- Level 2: Village-level burgundy (e.g., Gevrey-Chambertin)
- Level 3: First-growth (Premier Cru) burgundies from individual vineyards
- Level 4: Great-growth (Grand Cru) burgundies produced by the very best vineyards, exemplifying the best wine quality that Burgundy has to offer

In contrast to the leaner French burgundies, California Pinots are typically fruit-forward, juicy, and delicate. So which of these two wines do you prefer?

Sparkling Wines

By now you know how much I enjoy kicking off power entertaining events with the serving of champagne (or a close substitute) to guests. It surprises people and makes them feel special. So why not do a comparison tasting of sparkling wines at your next power entertaining dinner or reception?

In most people's minds, the greatest example of a sparkling wine is champagne from France, but many other countries produce sparkling wines as well. Italy produces Franciacorta and Prosecco; Germany, Sekt; Portugal, Espumante; and Spain, Cava. All of these sparkling wines come at a fraction of the price of French champagne!

Before we talk about comparison pairings, however, let me talk about how sparkling wine is produced. There are four principal production methods:

1. *Carbon Dioxide Injection:* This involves a simple injection of carbon dioxide (CO_2) into a base wine, which is the same process used for adding carbonation to soft drinks. This yields big bubbles that are hard on the palate and that dissipate quickly in a glass.

2. *Charmat Process:* During the Charmat process, sparkling wine undergoes a special secondary formation process in large tanks where it's bottled under pressure. Prosecco and Asti are both

made this way, which produces smaller, longer-lasting bubbles. The Charmat process is used all over the world to produce light, delicate sparkling wines.

3. *Transfer Method:* This method bottles sparkling wine for secondary fermentation, allowing for development of additional complexity, but then transfers the wine out of individual bottles into a larger tank after it has spent the desired amount of time on yeast.

4. *Traditional Method, or Méthode Champenoise:* This method creates superior and more complex sparkling wines through a secondary fermentation in the bottle. Invented in France, this technique is used to make champagne and other very high-quality sparkling wines in many parts of the world. In fact, whenever you see the terms *Méthode Champenoise, Méthode Traditionnelle, Méthode Classique,* or *Cremant* (the latter three in France), they indicate that the maker has followed a rigorous production process that the Champagne region invented. In Italy it is called *Metodo Classico,* and in South Africa it can be found on labels as *Cap Classique.*

Okay, now for two fun pairings of sparkling wines:

👍 Pairing #9: French Crémant versus German Sekt

This pairing of a French sparkling wine against a German sparkling wine makes for an interesting matchup. Sparkling wines designated Crémant are produced using the *traditional method* and have to adhere to strict production criteria. (For example, French winemaking regulations require that a Crémant be harvested by hand with yields not exceeding a set amount for their region. The wines must also be aged for a minimum of one year.) In France, there are seven appellations for sparkling wine that include the designation Crémant in their name. They include Crémant d'Alsace, Crémant de Bordeaux, Crémant de Bourgogne, Crémant de Die, Crémant du Jura, Crémant de Limoux, and Crémant de Loire.

Sekt is the German term for sparkling wine. The majority of Sekt produced (around 95 percent) is made by the Charmat method, with the remaining premium Sekt (5 percent) being made according to the Méthode Traditionnelle. Premium wines are typically made using Riesling, Pinot Blanc, Pinot Gris, or Pinot Noir grapes. A great deal of Sekt is consumed domestically by Germans rather than exported. In fact, Germans drink more sparkling wine per person than people in any other country in the world.

👍 **Pairing #10: Champagne Blanc de Blancs versus Champagne Traditional Cuvée**

In this pairing, sample two of the most famous styles of champagne from the Champagne region: blanc de blancs and traditional cuvée. *Blanc de blancs* (meaning "white of whites") is the term used to designate champagnes made exclusively from Chardonnay grapes. Blanc de blancs champagne is pure and focused, offering vibrant lime and tangerine flavors. Its finish in your mouth will include racy notes of wet stone and lime zest with chalky minerality. By contrast, traditional cuvée is made of Chardonnay, Pinot Noir, and Pinot Meunier grapes. This produces a sparkling wine known for its acidity and elegance, its structure and body, and its layers of aromatics.

Wines of the Pacific Northwest

Although most people know something about the fine wines of California, fewer are familiar with the wines of the Pacific Northwest, specifically Oregon and Washington State. Wines from this region are skyrocketing in popularity. So here are two wine pairings designed to showcase the wonderful regional attributes of these wines:

👍 **Pairing #11: Willamette Pinot Noir versus a Specific Willamette Subregion**

In winemaking there's an unwritten rule: "The more specific the site, the better the wine." That's never truer than when talking about Pinot Noir! So, for this pairing, ask your wine merchant to select a generic Willamette Pinot Noir to compare with a Pinot from one of the specific subregions in the Willamette Valley.

All Pinots from the Willamette Valley show remarkable elegance and are brimming with sour cherries, sweet mushrooms, and warm spices like cinnamon and cumin. That will be apparent in the generic Pinot chosen for this sampling. But then, see how your palate responds when you compare it to a Pinot produced in one of the specific sites in the Willamette Valley known for their assertive styles. This should be fun! As of today, there are six specific subregions in the Willamette Valley: Ribbon Ridge, McMinnville, Dundee Hills, Chehalem Mountain, Yamhill-Carlton District, and Eola-Amity Hills. These six sites have demonstrated their ability to produce wines of great complexity and character.

🖒 Pairing #12: Washington Merlot versus Washington Cabernet Sauvignon

Merlot often gets a bad rap—both from wine critics and wine drinkers alike. Although it's true that there are lots of mediocre Merlots out there (often made by winemakers more interested in producing Cabernet), there are winemakers who care deeply about making high-quality Merlot and many of them live and work in Washington State. As you'll see in this tasting, Washington Merlot is velvety soft and explodes on the palate with chocolate-covered plums, warm baking spices, and ripe tannins. It will delight you. Compare and contrast it to the Washington Cabernet in this pairing, whose cedary, black currant flavor will seduce your senses!

Cabernet Sauvignon

Cabernet Sauvignon is one of the world's best known red wine grape varieties. Grown in nearly all major wine-producing countries, it has become famous for its prominence in Bordeaux wines, where it is frequently blended with Merlot and Cabernet Franc. Cabernet Sauvignon is robust! Its body is full, its tannin level ranges from medium high to high, its acid level is medium to high, and its alcohol content is medium high to high. Cabernet Sauvignon can smell of fruits, specifically black currants, blackberries, and black cherries. It can also smell of nonfruits, including cedar, eucalyptus, licorice, mint, tobacco, and cigar box. Finally, it can smell of minerals, including black rocks, gravel, graphite, and pencil lead.

Cabernet Sauvignon is produced in a number of classic regions, including:

- Bordeaux: primarily the Left Bank
- California: Napa, Sonoma, Paso Robles, and others
- Washington State: Columbia Valley, Walla Walla, Yakima

It is also grown in:

- Australia: Margaret River, Coonawarra, Barossa Valley, Goulburn Valley, Beechworth, and elsewhere
- New Zealand: Hawks Bay, North Island
- South Africa: Breede River Valley and others
- Italy: Tuscany, Bolgheri

Cabernet grapes grow well in well-drained soils containing gravel and clay. Mountainsides and hilltops are typically best. The grapes prefer long warm growing seasons in moderate continental climates to achieve optimal ripeness. If harvested too early, Cabernet grapes are very vegetal and the tannins too sharp. If harvested too late, the flavors taste like canned fruits. Cabernet Sauvignon can be produced in various styles, ranging from earthy and cedary with lots of tobacco (in Bordeaux) to ripe and rich with minty notes in California, to super-ripe with lots of eucalyptus (used as wind breaks) in Australia.

Here are two must-do pairings of Cabernet Sauvignon to showcase the incredible variety and versatility of this amazing grape.

🔲 Pairing #13: Napa Valley versus Bordeaux

This is a blockbuster pairing if ever I designed one! The wines in this pair hark from what are, without question, the two most historic Cabernet-growing regions in the world: Napa Valley and Bordeaux.

The sun-drenched Napa Valley is home to some of the world's best wines, and Cabernet Sauvignon is the basis of many of them. It's amazing to think that this has been achieved in Napa in a relatively short time. After prohibition was repealed in 1933, it took the United States almost three and a half decades to take wine production seriously. In the 50 years since then, Napa Valley has attained legendary status for its Cabernets. At their core, Napa Valley Cabernets possess flavors and aromas of black currants, chocolate, and mint, among many others. The tannins are lively and rich, but well polished in the best examples. One of the great things about Napa Cabernet is that it is quite drinkable in its youth, but it benefits greatly from extended cellar aging.

As noted, the Bordeaux winemaking region of France is another home to great Cabernet Sauvignon. French Cabernets are typically blended with four other grapes to make up the famous quintet of Bordeaux varietals: Merlot, Cabernet Franc, Malbec, and Petite Verdot. (This blend of five grapes is called Meritage in California.) Winemakers will vary the blend percentages in order to ensure a high-quality product even in "off" years, when sunlight is scarce or rain persists. The wines grown in Bordeaux are more refined and restrained than their Napa Valley cousins. They show swirling dried red currants, violets, tobacco, and cedar aromas, and they typically require a little more cellar aging than their warmer climate, New World counterparts.

👍 Pairing #14: New Classic versus Old Classic

New classic and old classic comparisons are always fun, and in this pairing, I invite you to sample a specific subregional New World cabernet alongside a commune-specific Bordeaux from the Old World. Your local wine merchant or sommelier can help pick out specific wines to sample here, but mix things up a bit. In Napa Valley, from which you'll draw your New World classic for sampling, there are 17 separate subregions, each with its own unique terroir. Bordeaux, meanwhile, is composed of four different regions, each of which, in turn, is composed of subregions and villages that are vastly different from one another.

Cabernet Sauvignons display wonderful complexity, rich texture, and long-term aging potential. That's why they've become some of the most sought after wines in the world. This pairing shows you the specific depth and complexity of flavors that arise when tasting a specific subregional New World wine alongside a commune-specific Bordeaux from the Old World.

Merlot

Merlot is by far the most widely planted grape of the entire Bordeaux region. A highly drinkable wine, it is primarily made for blending, but it can be quite wonderful on its own and more approachable than any Cabernet on the planet. You just need to know where to look for it. (Château Petrus from Pomerol, one of the most sought after wines in the world, is more than 90 percent Merlot.) Merlot's body ranges from medium full to full. Its tannin is medium high. Its acid is medium high to high, and its alcohol content is medium. Merlot smells of nonfruits, including kalamata olives, anise, cocoa, bell peppers, and flowers, and of minerals, including granite and graphite. It tastes of plums, red cherries, and blackberries.

Merlot is produced in a number of classic regions, including:

- France: Bordeaux (the most widely planted varietal here), main component of the wines on the "Right Bank" (e.g., Pomerol, Lalande-de-Pomerol)
- California: Napa Valley, Sonoma Valley
- Washington State: Columbia Valley, Walla Walla

It's also grown in:

- Italy: Super Tuscans (like Massetto)
- California: pretty much everywhere
- Australia: Margaret River and Barossa Valley
- New Zealand: starting to have a bigger presence on the North Island

Merlot grapes like soils rich in volcanic clay, gravel, basalt, silt, and loess. Since Merlot is an early ripening grape, it thrives best in moderate to cool climates, where it can enjoy a long "hang time" to fully develop properly. It does not otherwise have the proper acidity and structure. Merlot can be made in many different styles from fruity and velvety to massively complex and tannic. If you enjoy Merlot it's important to seek out producers who enjoy making it as an end product. So let me suggest two pairings of Merlot wines to give you a broad view of this versatile and very popular wine.

👍 Pairing #15: Washington State Merlot versus Sonoma County, California, Merlot

In this pairing you see an example of the amazingly high-quality, terroir-driven Merlot that Washington State has to offer compared with a very delectable wine from one of the best Merlot-producing regions in California, Sonoma. You'll learn if you prefer the ultra-ripe, fruit-forward California style or the more "Bordeaux-like" Washington State expression.

👍 Pairing #16: Napa Valley versus Bordeaux

In this tasting I suggest you pair a New World Merlot against an Old World Merlot. Napa Valley Merlot is made of grapes picked at optimal ripeness. It is big and bold, with rich and powerful explosions of black cherry, plum, and coffee flavors, framed by a substantial amount of new French oak. Taste it, and you'll find it's like drinking silk! By contrast, Merlot from Bordeaux will be more refined and elegant, with high tannin and bright acid. Flavors of plum, tobacco, and graphite tend to dominate these wines.

California Wines

California is far and away the largest wine-producing state in the United States, and it produces a wide variety of quality wines. I suggest you get a good grounding in California's wine production practices, because it will give you insight into the nuances of California wines.

As in Europe, wine regions in the United States are identified based on geographic, geologic, and climatic similarities. Each American Viticultural Area (AVA), in theory, is thus highly likely to produce a similar style of wine when the same grape varietals are grown within the same region. The AVA system in the United States is modeled after the French AOP breakdown. Unlike Europe, however, the United States has no laws governing what can or cannot be grown in specific regions. Producers are free to grow any grapes they choose in any AVA and to put that AVA on the label as long as they meet certain legal criteria.

So what do you need to know here regarding California?

- In California, to use the "state" AVA of California on the label, 100 percent of the grapes must have been grown in California.
- For a producer to put an AVA on their label, a minimum of 85 percent of the grapes must have been grown in that AVA. (Unless it is a "county" AVA, in which case it is a 75 percent minimum.)
- For a producer to put a single vineyard on their label, 95 percent of the grapes must have been grown in that single vineyard.

Here are three paired tastings of California wines I suggest you try:

👍 Pairing #17: Napa Valley Chardonnay versus Santa Barbara

Napa Valley Chardonnay tends to be the richest, even flashiest style of chardonnay you taste from California. Most of these are generously oaked and go through full malolactic fermentation (deacidification/stabilization). Most winemakers in Napa also pick their grapes as late as possible to achieve optimal ripeness. This produces extremely fruit-forward wine with higher levels of alcohol. This is the type of Chardonnay that many Americans love.

Santa Barbara County chardonnays are more mineral-driven than those from Napa, often with little or no oak at all. This seems to be a growing trend in California Chardonnay production today. In Santa Barbara County Chardonnays, you see the pure expression of the varietal and get a clear sense of place. Winemakers in Santa Barbara tend to pick grapes earlier than those in Napa Valley to produce a more acidic, mineral-driven style of wine. But have no fear; the golden sunshine of the Central Coast still imparts plenty of ripe fruit flavors, even into Santa Barbara County wines. Look for the signature tropical fruit in these Chardonnays. You'll almost always be able to pick up the papaya, banana, and pineapple aromas that distinguish these wines.

👍 **Pairing #18: Pinot Noir: Russian River Valley versus Anderson Valley**

In this pairing we have a matchup of Pinots. The Russian River Valley AVA is a Sonoma County region that produces some of the most powerful yet still elegant Pinot Noir in California. The "classic" Russian River Pinot is very well balanced and offers sweet black cherry flavors accented with hints of spice and cola. If texture is what really excites your palate, Russian River Valley Pinot has it in spades.

If acid is more your thing, you may prefer the Anderson Valley Pinot. Anderson Valley produces some of the most delicate and aromatic Pinot Noirs in California. The style of a classic Anderson Valley Pinot Noir is very well proportioned, delivering fresh red berry flavors accented with white pepper and occasional hints of cedar. It displays a firm yet feminine structure with moderate oak influence, soft tannins, and a long finish.

👍 **Pairing #19: Cabernet Sauvignon: Napa Valley versus Sonoma County**

Napa Valley Cabernet Sauvignons possess flavors and aromas of black currants, chocolate, and mint (among other things). The tannins are lively and rich, but well polished in the best cases. One of the great things about Napa Cabernet is that it is quite drinkable in its youth but can benefit greatly from extending cellar aging.

Sonoma County Cabernet Sauvignons tend to be more elegant and acid-driven than Cabernet Sauvignon from Napa Valley. They also come across as more approachable, especially at a young age. These wines reflect more of the land in which they are grown, with notes of blackberry, red currant, blueberry, herbs, chocolate, and eucalyptus being most apparent.

German Wines

In my opinion, German wines, and especially Riesling, suffer from an image problem. Many Americans believe that all Riesling comes in blue bottles, is sweet, and is simple. That's not the case; the wine is far more interesting and versatile than its popular public image suggests, which I will demonstrate in a moment. But before I do, a few facts about German wine:

- German wines, when compared to other European wines, are produced in the most northerly region of Europe. Many of the vineyards are on very steep slopes, where they benefit from extra concentration of the sun's rays and reflected light from nearby rivers. It's a perfectly suited microclimate for growing Riesling, whose origins date back to 100 BC.

- The soil in this region consists of slate, shale, loam-loess, clay, sandstone, limestone, marl, volcanic pebbly gravel, and gypsum. Most sites are situated facing south for more sun exposure.

- There are 13 major winemaking regions ("Anbaugebiete") in Germany. They include Ahr, Baden, Franken, Hessische Bergstraße, Mittelrhein, Mosel-Saar-Ruwer, Nahe, Pfalz, Rheingau, Rheinhessen, Saale-Unstrut, Württemberg, and Sachsen.

Now, for some German wine terminology:

- *QbA (Qualitatswein—Quality Wine)* is the common classification for basic wines in Germany (much as AOC is the designation for such wines in France). Wines in this category range from Blue Nun on the low end to high-quality estate fruit wines from well-known producers. The main difference between wines of this category and wines of lesser quality is the allowance for chaptalization, that is, the addition of sugar during fermentation to increase alcohol and enhance the wine's flavor profile.

- *Pradikatswein (distinct wine, formerly known as QmP)* is the designation of a German wine of higher quality. Production of wines of this quality does not allow for chaptalization. They must be produced 100 percent naturally from the grape and have a hierarchy of quality that is based on ripeness levels at harvest.

The levels are explained below:

- *Kabinett* refers to wines whose grapes are picked during a normal harvest. This produces lighter-bodied, dry or semidry wines with relatively low alcohol levels (7 to 12 percent). These wines have an aging potential of three to five years.

- *Spätlese* is a term that means "late harvest" and identifies wines made from grapes picked late (7 to 12 days past the Kabinett) that are fully ripe, with greater intensity and strength. These wines are dry to fully sweet (alcohol content ranges from 8 to 13.5 percent), with bigger body and a more pronounced concentration of fruit. Their aging potential is 7 to 15-plus years.

- *Auslese* is the term for "selected harvest" and refers to wines made from very ripe grapes harvested in select bunches. These wines have a rich intensity and are produced only in the best warm years when *Botrytis* (a beneficial mold) can start to set in. These wines are much fuller in body than other wines and are loaded with tropical fruit aromas and balanced acidity. They are excellent as entry-level dessert wines but can also be made dry. Their aging potential is 25 to 40-plus years.

- *Beerenauslese* is a term that means "berry select" harvest. It refers to rare and costly wines that are deep and honeyed in flavor with a raisin richness. These wines have an aging potential of 60-plus years.

- *Trockenbeerenauslese* refers to wines that are derived from a dry, berry select harvest. They are the richest, sweetest, rarest, and most expensive wines in Germany and are made only in exceptional harvest years. Their alcohol content is normally 6 to 9 percent. They have an incredible richness and character to them. Their aging potential is 80-plus years.

- *Eiswein* is the designation of wines derived from very ripe frozen grapes. As the frozen grapes are pressed, the sweet, high acid concentrated juice is separated from the ice or water in the grape. This results in high levels of natural sugar and acidity. The aging potential of these wines is 100-plus years.

Note: As a general rule of thumb, if a wine is between 6 and 9 percent alcohol, it will be sweet; between 9 and 11.5 percent, off-dry; and north of 12 percent, typically dry. The more sugar left over after fermentation (residual sugar or RS), the greater the sweetness. The more sugar fermented to alcohol, the greater the dryness and the less the RS.

Okay, now for two enjoyable German wine pairings. Sampling German wines is fun because they differ significantly from wines of other countries. Take a look at what I've outlined as choices below to see if these pairings knock down some of the stereotypes you have about German wine!

👍 Pairing #20: Riesling: QbA (Dry) versus QmP Spätlese (Dry)

In this pairing I deliberately contrast two dry German wines: a dry Riesling called Mosel QbA and Spätlese. Mosel QbA (quality wine—dry) is commonly consumed as a house wine with the regional cuisine of Germany. It is an entry-level Riesling produced in all 13 major German wine-producing regions and can range in taste from dry to sweet. Spätlese is dry in style, even though the grapes used to make it are picked in late season. Contemporary German winemakers produce many versions of Spätlese in a dry style. In fact, today's German wine producers are making nearly 60 to 70 percent of their wines dry in style, but these usually don't get exported to the United States.

Although both of these wines are wonderful examples from their respective categories, there's a noticeable quality difference when they are tasted side by side. You should notice a greater depth of fruit and structure in the Spätlese.

👍 Pairing #21: Charta Association Riesling versus First-Growth Riesling

In this second German wine pairing, ask your sommelier to pick a Charta Association Riesling to pit against a first-growth Riesling. Here's a bit of history on why this wine pairing is significant. When it was founded in 1971, Germany's Wine Classification system didn't acknowledge the importance of the country's top wine-producing sites. Instead, designations of quality revolved around the sugar content in grapes at harvest time. In 1983 a group of wine producers founded the Charta Association to address this concern and to create a site-specific wine. In so doing, the Association put quality and production standards in place that far exceeded those of the German government at that time. Charta

Association (dry) Riesling reflects the high-quality standards of the Charta Association.

Subsequent to the creation of the Charta Association, the German government developed a similar set of new standards, known as the Erstes/Grosses Gewächs (first-/great-growth) wine classification system. Today, this system recognizes the top-quality wine-producing sites in Germany and holds these estates to exacting production standards. The second Riesling in this pairing, the first-growth Riesling, is one of these wines and reflects these high production standards.

When you taste these two wines side by side, notice that the Charta has a wonderful balance of acid and fruit, along with an extended finish. The first-growth Riesling has an even greater complexity and offers a stunning experience in a fuller-bodied dry Riesling. Both are wonderful additions to any social event or any power entertaining function you may want to put on.

Chablis

Ask any Master Sommelier what the truest expression of Chardonnay is, and they will most likely say, "Chablis, of course." Why's that? Well, you can start with Chablis's delightful "wet stone" bouquet. Then, there's the razor-sharp acidity, its steely body verging on metallic, green apple tartness, age-ability, and distinct terroir—all of which make Chablis a perennial favorite of many sommeliers!

Chablis is made in Chablis, a town in France at the northerly tip (coolest area) of the Burgundy region. The vineyards of this area are rich with a soil called Kimmeridgian clay, a mixture of clay, chalk, and oyster fossils, which helps give Chablis a distinctive "flintiness" of taste and a lean steeliness of body. Chablis vineyards are planted exclusively with Chardonnay grapes. That said, because of the cool climate of Chablis, Chablis wines display more acidity and less fruitiness than Chardonnay wines grown in warmer climates.

There are three distinct quality classifications of Chablis. They are distinguished mostly by the soil and slope conditions under which each is produced.

Chablis/Petite Chablis

Basic Chablis can be a true palate pleaser and a great representation of 100 percent French Chardonnay wine, particularly in the best vintages. That said, care must be taken when choosing from among producers, because the appellation covers a relatively large area. It encompasses many vineyards that don't get uniformly great sunlight and that therefore don't produce uniformly great product with the right balance of acidities and fruit. Your local wine merchant or sommelier can provide a wealth of wisdom and insight here, especially if you want to incorporate use of these wines into power entertaining events.

Premier Cru Chablis

The Premier Crus of Chablis are the next step up in quality from the basic Chablis designation. These are dry wines that vary from being light to fairly full bodied. They should always have a finer and longer finish than wines from the lower classifications of Chablis AOC and Petite Chablis. There are 40 Premier Cru vineyards scattered among 15 communes in Chablis. Again, the quality varies from producer to producer, so be sure to ask your sommelier or wine merchant for the names of the best producers.

Grand Cru Chablis

Grand Cru Chablis is the ultimate expression of Chablis. Seven vineyards in Chablis have Grand Cru status, along with another unofficial Grand Cru vineyard called La Moutonne. Each of these Grand Cru vineyards is located on the top of a hill (for maximum sun exposure) that overlooks the town of Chablis itself. The individual styles of these Grand Crus depend largely on how the winemaker vinifies and matures their wine. Grand Cru wines typically reflect a lot of oak, which adds to their complexity, yet some vintners age their wines only in stainless steel casks to preserve crispness. Grand Cru Chablis constitutes only 3 percent of all Chablis production. Collectors consider these white burgundies to be some of the finest "food wines" in the world, and they certainly are among my favorites to serve.

Here are the eight Grand Cru Chablis vineyards and what they're known for:

1. *Borgros*—vibrant; penetrating acidity
2. *Preuses*—vivid, expressive, and complex, with great finesse
3. *Vaudesir*—complex, intense flavors
4. *Grenouilles*—elegant and aromatic flavors
5. *Valmur*—fine bouquet; rich flavors
6. *Les Clos*—rich, luscious, and complex
7. *Blanchot*—floral; most delicate of the Grand Crus
8. *La Moutonne*—fine, long finish; expressive

Although a producer's style and vintage can play an influential role in determining the contours and character of a Chablis, only you can decide what kind of Chablis you prefer. I suggest that you try all three quality levels in a side-by-side tasting. Remember, you get what you pay for, so go for the best examples of each that you can afford.

👍 Pairing #22: Chablis versus Premier Cru

In this pairing choose a generic-quality Chablis to taste against a Chablis from a specific area. Generic-quality Chablis is a very pure expression of Chardonnay and will display flavors of green apples, lemon rind, chalk, straw, and pear skins in delightful combinations. Wines of the Chablis AOC experience only minimal oak aging in barrels, if any at all. By contrast, the Premier Cru will be more complex and multidimensional. Grapes in Premier Cru vineyards are given longer to mature during the course of a vintage than is the case in other vineyards. The added time on the vine increases the complexity and character of these Chablis, making them richer in texture and more memorable and nuanced in flavor. You'll notice this when tasting a Premier Cru. The scents are more distinctive in the glass than is the case with regular Chablis. Another distinguishing characteristic of Premier Cru is the length of time that the wine stays on your palate. Its finish lingers.

🔖 Pairing #23: Premier Cru versus Grand Cru

This is the matchup of Chablis you've been waiting for! As noted, Premier Crus are lovely wines of elegance and finesse; their flavors are pure, expressive, and complex. But there's really no comparison to Grand Cru. The seven Grand Cru vineyards of Chablis are, in reality, one contiguous strip of land that is separated into seven distinct terroirs (eight if you include La Moutonne). These vineyards are the last to be harvested each year and thus produce the most powerful wines of Chablis. The true mark of a Grand Cru is the length of its finish. Sample Grand Cru and see how long the finish lingers and the flavor continues to evolve. You'll experience a symphony of flavor and nuances, which is what makes great wine great!

As you offer guests this pairing, challenge them to articulate the distinctions they perceive between the Premier Cru and Grand Cru. Which do people prefer, and why? What adjectives do they use to describe each wine as they taste it?

Italian Wines

Discovering the pleasures of the rustic food wines of Italy is something that could take the rest of your life! The truth is most people simply don't have the time or inclination to do this, and here's why: in Italy there are 20 different wine regions, 361 authorized grape varieties, and 300-plus growing zones with accompanying wine laws that are so complex that I don't want to confuse you with them.

All that said, I feel strongly that you should have a solid understanding of two of the most important wine regions in Italy, because wines from these regions are very likely to show up on restaurant wine lists. The two regions are the northern region of Piedmont and the region of Tuscany. A firm understanding of the stars from both regions will give you all the ammunition you need to power entertain impressively with Italian wines.

The Wines of Piedmont

The wines of Piedmont are the most famous of all Italian red wines. The winemakers of Piedmont use winemaking techniques that are evocative of Burgundy in that they emphasize a single grape variety (Nebbiolo) and focus on showcasing the aromatics and earthiness (terroir) of specific vineyard sites. As a grape, Nebbiolo displays a full-bodied, highly alcoholic, extreme tannic, and intensely flavored style when made into wine. Because of this, Nebbiolo wines need some aging (at least 5 to 10 years) to become well balanced. The best of them can be aged 50 years or longer. Nebbiolo wines have flavors suggestive of rose petals, tar, truffles, violets, and dark red fruits.

The suggested pairing follows:

👍 Pairing #24: Barolo versus Barbaresco

The two most important Nebbiolo-based wines to be familiar with are Barolo and Barbaresco. Thus, I recommend a tasting that pairs these two wine partners together. (FYI, Barolo produces bigger wines than Barbaresco.) Ask your sommelier to come up with a pairing of these two wines using the best wines of both types that you can afford. Be sure the wines are of equal quality and vintage; this will enable you to clearly see the differences between these two stars.

Table 6.1 is a list of Italian communes that produce Barolo and Barbaresco, along with their important Crus.

TABLE 6.1 Barolo and Barbaresco Communes

Barolo Commune	Important Crus
Barolo	Cannubi, Brunate (shared), Sarmassa
La Morra	Brunate (shared), Cerequio, Le Rocche
Serralunga d'Alba	Lazzarito, Cerretta
Castiglione Falletto	Bricco Rocche, Monprivato, Villero, Bricco Fiasco
Monforte d'Alba	Bussia, Ginestra, Santo Stefano
Barbaresco Commune	**Important Crus**
Barbaresco	Asili, Roncagliette, Martinenga, Rabaja
Nieve	Serraboella, Gallina, Basarin
Treiso	Pajore, Bricco di Treiso

In choosing Barolo and Barbaresco wines to sample and enjoy, here are some specific wine producers whose vineyards and wines you should investigate:

- Angelo Gaja
- Giacomo Conterno
- Bruno Giacosa
- Giacomo Borgogno, Massolino
- Vietti

If the preceding wines are a bit beyond your budget, there are other more affordable and ready-to-drink Nebbiolos to be found in an area called Langhe in the heart of Piedmont. Here, in this "region within a region," hundreds of vineyards are nestled amid medieval castles that have overlooked rolling fields of grapes for centuries. Many of the Nebbiolo-based wines that come out of this area are blended with Syrah and Cabernet Sauvignon to soften them. Look for the 100 percent Nebbiolo versions from Produttori del Barbaresco. These are excellent and reasonably priced restaurant wines. Two other reasonably priced Nebbiolo-based wines that you often see on good wine lists are Gattinara and Ghemme. They represent good value. Finally, a favorite of mine is Spanna, which is made predominantly of Nebbiolo, Vespolina, and Bonarda grapes.

Other red grapes from Northern Italy to be familiar with are Barbera and Dolcetto. Barbera produces lighter, medium-bodied wines with less aggressive tannins compared with Barolo and Barbaresco. They have a rustic earthiness, and restaurants like to stock them because of their cutting acidity and affordable prices. Dolcetto is a much lighter-style red with notes of sweet black fruits and bright acidity. It goes perfectly with pizza.

👍 Pairing #25: Barbera versus Dolcetto

Do a side-by-side tasting of Barbera and Dolcetto to identify their differences. To do this, put yourself in the hands of a competent sommelier as these wines range in quality from being one-dimensional to brilliant. As always, you get what you pay for!

Finally, still another powerful red (from the Veneto region) is Amarone della Valpolicella, or simply Amarone. This wine, produced from Corvina and Rondinella grapes, is characterized by extremely ripe cherry and bittersweet almond/mocha flavors. These wines taste their best with 7 to 10 years of aging and go well with heavy roasts and game.

Italian White Wines of the North

When it comes to my favorite Italian whites, I suggest you try Gavi (Cortese di Gavi or Gavi di Gavi). This wine is made from the Cortese grape and is dry, mineral-tinged, and a great companion to seafood. Also, try Roero, a fresh and floral wine made from the Arneis grape, which makes for a great apéritif.

Often you will see two common white wines from Veneto on wine lists: Soave and Pinot Grigio. I suggest you pass on these, as most of them are mass-produced, with little varietal distinction (with the exception of Pieropan Soave). I feel the same about the Verona reds (Bardolino and Valpolicella). These show up on most wine lists and are light-bodied Beaujolais-style wines with little distinction. There are exceptions, and a good sommelier can show you these.

Wines of Tuscany

The other important red wine region dominating Italian wine lists is Tuscany. The four wines that appear everywhere from Tuscany are:

1. Chianti
2. Chianti Classico
3. Brunello di Montalcino
4. Super Tuscans

Sangiovese (aka Brunello) is the main grape variety of Tuscany. This grape produces earthy, light-colored, medium-bodied wines with high acidity, firm tannins, and a note of sour cherries and herbal undertones. Because the region of Chianti is synonymous with Italy, there is a plethora of producers making innocuous, highly acidic wines that are inexpensive and unimpressive. You'll definitely need help from your wine merchant or sommelier to show you what to look for here.

▣ Pairing #26: Chianti versus Chianti Classico

For fun, do a paired tasting of basic Chianti and its subregion wine, Chianti Classico. Basic Chianti is composed of approximately 75 percent (or more) Sangiovese grapes blended with red grapes of Canaiolo and/or Cabernet Sauvignon. By comparison, Chianti Classico wines are required to have at least 85 percent Sangiovese. What distinctions do you draw in tasting these two wines side by side?

Super Tuscans

Back in the 1970s, certain winemakers made an attempt to soften the edge of their Sangiovese-based wines by blending in Bordeaux varietals like Cabernet Sauvignon and Merlot. The resulting wines, not conforming to the traditional Sangiovese recipe, became known as Super Tuscans. Although many impressive wines have resulted from this blending, including Tignanello, Sassicaia, Ornellaia, and Solaia, they don't resemble Chianti at all. That's because they are more New World (fruit-forward) in style in response to market demand. Italian Syrah is also being blended this way now.

One Super Tuscan I like very much is Brunello di Montalcino, produced from the Sangiovese look-alike Sangiovese Grosso (Brunello). This wine is aged in a cask for a minimum of two years and in the bottle for four to six months for the *Riserva*. Brunello represents the ultimate expression of Sangiovese, being more tannic than Chianti. These are pricey wines that need at least five to seven years of aging before reaching their peak of flavor.

Other reasonably priced Tuscany wines to search out on restaurant wine lists include:

- Carmignano (minimum 50 percent Sangiovese blended with Cabernet Sauvignon and Cabernet Franc)

- Vernaccia di San Gimignano (the only classified Tuscan white wine; has a slightly pink color with crisp, refreshing acidity)

Spanish Wines

Today, Spain is the third largest wine producer in the world. There are more than 70 different wine regions (designated Demoninaciónes di Origin, or DOs) for you to experience. But to keep things simple (at least initially), ask your local sommelier or wine merchant for an overview of what they consider the most important Spanish winemaking regions and grape varieties. Following are some of the regions with which you should be familiar.

Rioja

Rioja is perhaps Spain's most famous region, and its wines are found on all good wine lists. Tempranillo is the predominant grape variety, often blended with Graciano, Garnacha (Grenache), and Mazuelo (Carignan) grapes. One of the most popular wines that comes out of Rioja is Tempranillo, a medium to full-bodied wine recognized for having flavors of dark berries such as plum and cherry and a rustic earthiness akin to leather or cigar box. Another Rioja favorite is Garnacha, a wine that's often fuller-bodied, contributing deep-colored jamminess along with a hint of black pepper.

The wines of Rioja are subject to more oak aging than other Spanish wines. You'll see on the back label just how much aging each wine undergoes before being released. Terms to be aware of include:

- Gran Reserva—5 years of age (2 years in oak barrels)
- Reserva—3 years of age (1 year in oak barrels)
- Crianza—2 years of age (1 year in oak barrels)

👍 **Pairing #27: Crianza versus Gran Reserva**

A fun wine pairing is to compare Crianza and a Gran Reserva to see the effect of age/oak.

Ribera del Duero

Wines from Ribera del Duero (150 miles southwest of Rioja) come from a warmer region, which leads to reds with a more powerful style than wines from Rioja. As in Rioja, Tempranillo is the dominant grape variety, often blended with Garnacha. In some respects the wines of this region are being produced today like the Super Tuscans of Italy with Cabernet Sauvignon, Malbec, and Merlot grapes, often blended together to create untraditional Western-style "fruit-forward" wines. My suggestion is that you have your somm conduct side-by-side wine tastings of Old World and New World styles so that you can decide which style you prefer.

One of the greatest wines from Ribera del Duero that I have ever tasted is the 1968 Vega Sicilia Unico, arguably Spain's most famous wine. A few years ago I took my daughter Elissa and a bottle of 1968 Vega Sicilia Unico to visit my friend and fellow Master Sommelier Nunzio Alioto at his restaurant, Alioto's on Fisherman's Wharf in San Francisco. As we tasted the wine he said to me, "Eddie, can any bottle of wine on the planet taste better than this wine does now?" After tasting it herself, my daughter called a friend back at Cornell, where she was a student and told him, "I just tasted the finest bottle of wine in my life!" After she had hung up, Nunzio leaned forward and said to her, "Young lady, I want you to know that this specific bottle of wine may be the very best wine you will *ever* taste in your life!"

Rias Baixas

The Rias Baixas wine region is famous for one of Spain's most famous white wines: Albariño. This wine comes from the northwest region of Galicia, which borders the Atlantic coast. It's a great choice when I am looking for a crisp, high-acid wine for shellfish. These wines vary in quality, so ask your somm for help in finding one to sample.

Valdeorras

The Valdeorras region is 100 miles inland from the Atlantic coast, where the soil is as hard as rock, requiring the roots of vines to extend themselves deep into the ground. Valdeorras is where Godello (pro-nounced go-day-o) is produced. Godello is my favorite Spanish white. It is medium bodied with a lovely wildflower nose and has bracing acidity that gives it a long finish. It possesses the minerality of a good Chablis and is the perfect accompaniment to all shellfish. Look for the unoaked versions.

Rueda

Rueda, consisting of 52 vineyards or "bodegas," produces a nice white wine, Verdejo, that you'll often see on good wine lists. Made of a grape by the same name, Verdejo is characterized by a citrusy minerality that makes it a natural partner to all seafood. Most Verdejo is reasonably priced. Taste one next to an Albariño and see which one you like.

Toro

The Toro region, just a short distance from the Portuguese border, is an extremely rural wine region known for its robust red wines. One wine from this region, Toro (named for the town of Toro), has cap-tured the attention of many lovers of Spanish wine. The wine is made predominantly from Tempranillo (locally Tinto de Toro), and some of the best are "purebred"—that is, 100 percent from that one grape. In other cases, Toro will also include Garnacha and Cabernet Sauvignon. Popular examples of Toro are dark, extremely intense, jammy, and, in my opinion, a bit too strong to be paired with much of Spain's elegant cuisine. Try pairing this wine with barbecued smoked ribs instead!

Priorato

Finally, there's the region of Priorato. Priorat wines are made from Cariñeña (Carignan) and Garnacha (Grenache) grapes. The moun-tainous Priorato region is south of Barcelona and is composed of granite-like soils that force the roots of the vines to search deeply for water. This stresses the vines and causes them to have low yields, deep colors, and intense flavors with a unique minerality. Harsh growing conditions, low-yielding vines, and use of new French oak barrels make these wines a bit on the expensive side. New winemaking techniques are being used in this region (blending Cabernet Sauvignon, Merlot, and Syrah). I suggest, however, that you stick to time-tested Old World earthy styles of these wines to get a true sense of this region's terroir. The "high-test" versions of these wines that are now being made lack the pedigree of the earthy Old World styles.

Rhône Wines

Wines from the Rhône Valley, south of Burgundy, can be broken down into Northern Rhônes and Southern Rhônes. In the north, Syrah is the dominant red grape. Its personality can be described as full-bodied, opaque, spicy (black pepper), gamey (meat), rustic, and earthy. The most famous Northern Rhônes that you'll find on all good wine lists include:

- Côte-Rôtie (roasted slope)
- Hermitage
- Cornas

All three of these wines are truly world-class wines (with prices to match), depending on who is producing them. So get your somm's recommendations on what to buy and sample.

Three other reasonably priced wines from the Northern Rhône offer extraordinary pleasure. Make sure you try them. They are:

1. Crozes-Hermitage
2. Saint-Joseph
3. Saint-Peray

Last, there's a very good white wine from the Condrieu appellation that is made from the Viognier grape. Viognier produces wines with a honeyed lushness, intriguing floral aromas, and rich textures. The best of them are stunning and pricey.

The Southern Rhônes are mostly Grenache-based and are richly jammy. The most famous Southern Rhône wine is Châteauneuf-du-Pape (aka CDP), whose quality ranges from one-dimensional to superb, with concentrated layers of fruit. You need the help of your somm to pick the right one of these. The best CDPs can be astonishing. One of my favorite restaurants Rhônes is called Gigondas, from the town of the same name. These are often some of the best values on restaurant wine lists.

Chilean, Argentinean, and South African Wines

The wines from Chile and Argentina offer some respectable wines at reasonable prices. In Chile, Cabernet Sauvignon and Carmenère are the major red grape varieties, as well as Chardonnay. In Argentina, Cabernet Sauvignon and Malbec are the dominant reds. Malbec is a great choice with grilled steak. Be sure to ask the advice of your somm or wine merchant, because the variations in quality are all over the board. Argentina also produces a white wine called Torrontés, which is a light-bodied, medium dry wine with citrusy aromas. It can be a nice apéritif wine when made well.

Portugal

The most popular white wine seen on wine lists in Portugal is Vinho Verde. It is made from the Alvarinho grape variety. This wine is light-bodied, vibrantly acidic, and great with shellfish. The climate is very warm in Portugal, and thus the country also produces some powerful reds. In my opinion, the best red grape variety is Touriga Nacional. The best wines made from this grape are intensely fruity and very tannic.

South Africa

South Africa produces excellent wines. On a recent trip with my fellow Master Sommeliers, we enjoyed some bone-dry Chenin Blanc (called Steen) from this region. Lovely! The country's Sauvignon

Blanc is very successful and sometimes exhibits both New World fruit and Old World minerality. Also, check out South Africa's wonderful sparkling wines, as well as its Cabernet Sauvignon, Shiraz, and Pinot Noirs. One varietal that's unique to South Africa is Pinotage, which is a hybrid of Pinot Noir and another variety called Hermitage (aka Cinsault). For samples of each wine I've described here, seek out the help of a qualified sommelier.

Other Wines

- *Grüner Veltliner:* This is a wine from Austria that is light and dry to fruity, with good acid that distinguishes itself from other white varieties with overtones of radish and white pepperiness.
- *Alsace whites:* Alsace is located in the northwest part of France. The region is dry and gets lots of sun. The best vineyards face south, allowing for maximum ripeness in most vintages. This environment produces medium to full-bodied wines that partner extremely well with food. Alsace whites are some of my favorite restaurant whites because of the consistently good vintages available at reasonable prices. Four grape varieties are planted in the region's Grand Cru vineyards, including:

    a. Riesling

    b. Pinot Gris

    c. Muscat

    d. Gewürztraminer

    There are currently 51 Grand Cru vineyards in Alsace, and you should definitely get acquainted with the wines of these Grand Crus. One of my favorite memories is of sharing a glass of bone-dry Muscat with my daughter Elissa on the bank of the river in front of the famous three-star Auberge de L'lll in Colmar.

- *Australian wines:* The best wines in Australia are produced in the southern, more temperate regions suitable for grape growing. The most important Australian grape varieties seen on restaurant wine lists today are Chardonnay, Riesling, Shiraz (Syrah), and Cabernet Sauvignon. The most important wine-growing regions in Australia include:

Western Australia

- ○ Margaret River

South Australia

- ○ Barossa Valley
- ○ Clare Valley
- ○ McLaren Vale
- ○ Coonawarra

Victoria
New South Wales

- ○ Hunter Valley

Other grape varieties planted all over Australia are Merlot, Mourvèdre, Grenache, Viognier, Sémillon, and Muscat.

- *New Zealand:* The three most important New Zealand varietals you'll see on restaurant wine lists are Sauvignon Blanc, Chardonnay, and Pinot Noir. Ask your somm for help in selecting New Zealand wines to sample from the following wine growing regions:

North Island

- ○ Gisborne
- ○ Hawke's Bay
- ○ Wairarapa/Wellington

South Island

- ○ Marlborough
- ○ Central Otago

- *Greece:* Space precludes me from saying as much about Greek wines as I'd like to, but I do want to say something about Domaine Sigalas. This is a property of vineyards on the volcanic island of Santorini. I had the opportunity to visit this site with a group of my fellow Master Sommeliers, and the wines produced there are extraordinary. They're made from the Assyrtiko grape. Domaine Sigalas makes "no oak" versions of its wines as well as barrel-aged versions. We tasted barrel-aged wines 15 years old that had extraordinary minerality with bracing acidity levels. These are go-to wines for grilled seafood. Yum!

Fortified Wines

The three most important fortified wines found on most wine lists are sherry, port, and Madeira. Fortified wines are produced with the addition of alcohol, hence fortifying them. The addition of alcohol generates fuller-bodied wines that fall in the range of 17 to 22 percent alcohol. Fortified wines range from bone-dry (Sercial Madeiras, Fino sherries) to richly sweet (Malmsey Madeira and Pedro Ximenéz sherry), making them some of the best apéritif and dessert wines.

Here is a snapshot of the basic styles of each. Ask your sommelier to design pairings of these so that you can familiarize yourself with them.

Sherry (Spain)

Sherry made from the Palomino grape distinguishes itself by being deliberately oxidized in the production process. There are two different types of sherry: Fino and Oloroso. *Fino*s are light-bodied and have a distinct nutty aroma coming from yeast whereas *Olorosos* are rich and full-bodied and oxidized without yeast.

Fino-Style Sherries

Following are the four fino-style sherries available:

1. *Fino sherry:* These are light and crisp apéritif wines (drunk as an appetizer before a meal). Finos are perfect with salty tapas. They should be served well chilled to avoid any alcoholic burn. (Unfortunately, in America, you often find them sitting on the bar at room temperature!) They are fragile and should be consumed within a day or so once opened.

2. *Manzanilla Sherry:* This is a Fino-style Sherry. These sherries are made from grapes that come from the seacoast, where sea breezes contribute a salty tanginess to their flavor. The result is that these sherries amplify the taste of foods with which they are served. Try this sherry with oysters, and you'll see a classic gastronomic marriage.

3. *Amontillado sherry:* Here you have the fullest-bodied Fino-style sherry. They are darker, older, harder to make (more expensive) and higher in alcohol (17 to 22 percent) than other sherries.

4. *Palo Cortado:* This is a rare variety of sherry (accounting for only 2 percent of annual sherry production) that is produced accidentally during the aging/oxidizing process, rendering it somewhere between a Fino and an Oloroso. It's one of my favorite sherries because it possesses the crisp acidity of an Amontillado as well as the richness of an Oloroso. Seek this out. It makes a great client gift!

Oloroso-Style Sherries

Following are the main Oloroso-style sherries available:

- *Oloroso sherry:* These are distinctly different from the Fino-style sherries. The best of them are considerably older (hence the dark gold colors) and often blended with other vintages to give them a walnut or caramel flavor.

- *Cream sherry:* This is a heavy, sweet style of sherry made from Pedro Ximenéz grape concentrate. It's too cloying for me.

- *Pedro Ximenéz (PX) sherry:* This is the sweetest of all sherries. It is made from the Pedro Ximenéz grape, which is traditionally used to add sweetness and color to other sherries. These sherries are almost black in color, with a cloyingly caramelized sweetness. They make a great topping on ice cream!

Port (Portugal)

There are two basic styles of ports: those aged in wood and those aged in bottles. Ports aged in wood mature more quickly, many being fully mature upon release. Bottle-aged port (vintage port) ages very slowly, and many of them need at least 20 years of aging before they express their true complex personalities. Here's more:

- *Ruby port:* This is a wood-aged port that is uncomplicated, deeply colored, one-dimensional in flavor, and characterized by an alcoholic fieriness if served at room temperature (which, unfortunately, most of them are). I describe this as entry-level port.

- *Tawny port:* This is smooth-tasting aged ruby port (three years in the barrel). These have a tawny color due to the oxidative aging process. A good friend of mine, an Episcopalian, tells me his congregation uses Tawny port as their Communion wine of choice.

- *Aged Tawny ports:* In these ports, you start to see complexity as they are aged considerably and offered in 10-, 20-, 30-, and 40-year-old blends. Ask your somm to do a side-by-side comparison of a 10-year Tawny with a 30- or 40-year Tawny to see a fascinating evolution of flavors.

- *Late-bottled vintage (LBV) port:* These are aged four to six years in casks before being bottled. They are always made from one vintage. What distinguishes them from vintage ports is that they have undergone more barrel aging and are mature on release, making them ideal restaurant selections.

- *Vintage port:* These are the ports of collectors and represent just 2 percent of overall port production. They are aged in bottles as opposed to wood casks and are produced by port houses only in exceptional harvest years. To give you some context here, a typical port producer (house) will declare only a vintage port three times in a decade. These wines will last a human lifetime, most of them needing at least 20 years to begin to achieve balance and complexity. They are very expensive. Ask your somm to let you taste several vintages side by side to see the mellowing effects of age.

- *Single Quinta port:* These ports emanate from the harvest of one estate. Sometimes when a port house doesn't feel confident enough to declare a vintage port, it will choose to release a Single Quinta port from one of its estates instead. They require much less aging, making them a wise restaurant choice. Try one of these next to a vintage port to see the subtle (or big) differences, depending on your experience.

Madeira (Portugal)

Madeira is an island 500 miles off the coast of Portugal. There you can find some of the most fascinating wines in the world. The wines of this island originally developed their oxidative style because as island residents traveled by ship along tropical trade routes, the wines they carried with them endured excessive temperatures. The wines survived these temperatures but were essentially cooked in ships' holds. Characteristics like burned toffee with tangy acidity were the result. Today these wines are heated during the production process to mimic the heat of a tropical journey (much more economical). The result is wines that are virtually indestructible and capable of being aged for hundreds of years.

There are four styles of Madeira, each named after a specific grape variety:

1. *Sercial:* This is the only dry-style Madeira. It is citrusy with an almond bouquet. It is my favorite apéritif wine to offer clients and friends because most people have never experienced it. Serve it well chilled.

2. *Verdelho:* This grape produces a fuller-bodied wine than Sercial. It has a smoky, slightly honeyed character.

3. *Bual (aka Boal):* This richer style of Madeira has a hint of sweetness that plays against vibrant acidity. I love serving this wine because it has one of the longest aftertastes you will ever experience.

4. *Malmsey:* This is the sweetest Madeira available, although it still has great acidity. Notes of toffee, vanilla, and marmalade explode from the best of them. Serve it with nuts, cheese, and dried fruits (apricots).

Multivintage Blends

Often you will see each of the grape varieties just described offered as 5-, 10-, 15-, and 30-year blends. Have your somm pour you a 5-year-old Madeira next to a 15-year-old Madeira, and you will fully understand why the 15-year bottle is more expensive. You *must* do this!

Vintage Madeira

Two vintage Madeiras are:

1. *Colheita:* Colheita Madeira is produced from a single vintage (85 percent minimum is required) and aged five years prior to bottling. Colheita is a good restaurant choice because it offers vintage Madeira without the extended cask aging and expense of a true vintage Madeira.

2. *Frasqueira:* This is vintage Madeira aged for a minimum of 20 years in casks. These wines are often further aged, sometimes decades in glass demijohns, after aging in casks. Frasqueira is the epitome of Madeira, very expensive and something you absolutely must get a taste of in your exploration of the finest wines in the world.

Want to do something special? Visit the island of Madeira. I did, and it was like going back in time 60 years. To this day it is my most memorable vacation with my family.

Premium Sake

Sake (pronounced sock-ee) is a popular Japanese alcoholic beverage that is often referred to as rice wine. Like wine and beer, it is a fermented beverage, derived, in sake's case, from starches in certain forms of rice such as sakamai that are then converted into sugar. What makes sake different from either beer or wine is that the conversion of starch to sugar and then sugar to alcohol occurs simultaneously in the same tank. In that tank, yeasts combine with a very special cultured mold called koji to ferment into the final product.

There are more than 1,300 sake breweries in Japan. When produced, sake ranges in strength from 15 to 17 percent alcohol. The four grades of premium sake are legally defined by how much the rice has been milled before fermentation (see Figure 6.4). The more the rice is milled, the cleaner, lighter, and more delicate the flavor of the sake—and the higher its price! *Super premium sakes* generally run in the retail range of $20 to $60 a bottle. The best *Daiginjo sake* (like premium wine) can cost more than $100 a bottle.

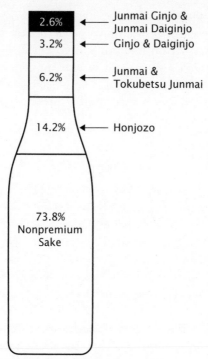

FIGURE 6.4   The Anatomy of Sake

Premium sake tastes best when slightly chilled. The traditional practice of heating sake will destroy the delicate nature of premium sake yet can mask the flaws of lower-quality sakes. Premium sake begins to oxidize once opened, so don't keep it longer than a day or so. Sake is meant to be drunk young, as it does *not* improve with age. Sake is also meant to be served with food. (You don't see real sake enthusiasts drinking sake by itself.)

When pairing sake with foods, think as you do with wines. Take the robust, fuller-bodied Junmai and match it with foods of similar weight and intensities (grilled Kurobuta pork, soy-infused ribs, etc.). When enjoying the lighter, more elegant Daiginjo, look for more delicate foods to pair it with, such as sashimi, broiled fish, lobster, crab, and oysters. All sake is too delicate to do well with spicy foods.

To learn more about the wonderful world of sake, here's a website I recommend you visit: www.sake-world.com. Learn from

John Gauntner, the world's leading non-Japanese sake expert. He has written three excellent books, which you'll find on his website. He also offers a three-day professional sake course in the United States and in Japan. Another site to visit is www.vineconnections.com. It's loaded with information about sake. This California-based importer is the exclusive US representative for some of the world's most unique wines and Japanese sake.

Beer

Why am I including a section about beer in a book about wine? Simple. Sometimes beer is a better option when trying to pair bold and spicy dishes that often overwhelm delicate wines. As a power entertainer, your goal should be to create memorable experiences for your guests by offering different kinds of libation—in some cases, beers—which your clients or friends have never heard of.

This is easy to do! Why do I say that? Because if you take a casual look inside most people's refrigerators, what you see there as far as beer goes is pretty boring. There's typically a random selection of light beers as well as the usual cast of nationally advertised brands and you know what they are. So all you have to do is get ahold of some specialty beers when you have company over, or when you want to showcase beer at a business event. Do this, and it will set you apart from almost everybody else.

Awhile back, I attended a course at the University of California, Davis, titled "Sensory Evaluation of Beer for Microbrewers" conducted by the dynamic team of Professor Michael J. Lewis and his associate Jean-Xavier Guinard. One of the most important things they emphasized about beer was that the flavor of beer starts to deteriorate as soon as it leaves the brewery. For that reason it's important to consume beer when it is as fresh and as close to its production site as possible. The best way to do this is at the brewery itself. And that's why true beer lovers have fallen in love with microbreweries and brewpubs all over the United States. This is where beer is at its freshest!

When I entertain and have chosen to serve beer to guests, I always go to my favorite local brewpub and bring home assorted ales and lagers in half-gallon growlers. I highly recommend you do the same, because few people do; thus it's easy to impress both clients and friends!

The flavor profile of most beers is determined by the inter-play between sweetness (malt-pale or roasted) and bitterness (hops-aromatic or bitter). The degree of bitterness in a beer (which results from acid in hops) is measured in International Bittering Units (IBUs). Those who prefer high IBU beers are called hopheads!

Ales and Lagers

There are two major styles of beers: ales and lagers. Ales are made with quickly fermenting top-fermenting yeasts that prefer warmer temperatures, which results in higher-alcohol and richer beers. Lagers are made with slower bottom-fermenting yeasts that prefer cooler temperatures, which results in lower-alcohol, crisply refresh-ing beers.

The five styles of ales include:

1. *Pale ale:* These are usually bronze or copper-colored as opposed to dark brown.
2. *Bitters:* These have good acidity and a hoppy bitterness in the finish.
3. *Porters:* These are dark in color and strong in flavor but lighter than stouts.
4. *Stouts:* These are extra dark, almost black in color and made with highly roasted malts.
5. *Wheat (or Weisse):* These are made from wheat and have a tart spicy taste.

There are two styles of lagers:

1. *Pilsner:* These are classic beers, golden in color with a flowery aroma and dry finish.
2. *Bock:* This is a German term for a strong beer, high in alcohol (12-plus percent) with rich malty characteristics

Chapter Wrap-Up

In this chapter I've thrown a lot of material at you, and at this point you probably feel as if you've been drinking from a fire hose! But fear not; this isn't a test. The ideas I've given you here are simply suggestions about what to serve at power entertaining events. I hope you'll take the time to try these suggestions and experiment with others. In any case, this chapter should be a huge help to you, be it in talking intelligently with wine merchants and sommeliers or in thinking about what kinds of wines and beers to serve at power entertaining functions. Hopefully, by reading this chapter, you've also grown in your knowledge and appreciation of wine and know how to compare and contrast wines across vintages.

7

Taste Wine like the
Masters Do

I learned at l'Institut d'Oenologie, Bordeaux that your sense of taste is as unique as your fingerprints. What you experience with your tongue is different from everybody elses. So you have to learn to go with your instincts.

—Eddie O.

I'm assuming that since you're reading this book, you're a wine lover, somebody who enjoys hoisting a glass to your lips on a regular basis—be it at home after a hard day at work or in celebration and camaraderie with friends, family, and business colleagues. I'm also assuming that power entertaining others is part of your formal (or informal) job description, as we discussed in Chapter 1. Finally, I'm assuming that although you personally enjoy wine and perhaps even fancy yourself a collector or wine connoisseur, you probably don't know as much about it as you'd like to and would like to become more familiar with how to taste, sample, and savor wine when you drink it.

For all these reasons, this chapter introduces you to the finer points of wine tasting and wine appreciation. My goals are to help you increase your own enjoyment of wine and to be able to share your newfound knowledge and appreciation of wine with others in power entertaining situations.

Demystifying Wine

To many people, the subtleties and distinctions of wine drinking remain something of a mystery. Even today, although wine is enjoyed by far more people than was the case a few decades ago, the world of wine appreciation can still seem a little esoteric and snooty at times, the apparent domain of self-professed wine connoisseurs and food snobs, as well as rich suburbanites and the uptown urban elite. I want you to put all those stereotypes of wine drinkers aside, because they simply aren't accurate. Wine drinking and wine appreciation are for *everybody!*

That said, there are some things to learn about the tasting and appreciation of wine that you probably never knew before but that can enhance your experience of wine in wonderful new ways.

A Systematic Approach to Wine Tasting

A lot of people find it hard to express the feelings and sensations they have when they drink a glass of wine. This is only natural unless you've had formal training in the study of wine and winemaking. Given that reality, let me introduce you to a systematic approach to wine tasting that I learned while a student of Dr. Emile Peynaud at l'Institut d'Oenologie, Bordeaux, years ago. A legendary figure in the world of wine for several decades, Professor Peynaud used to talk about wine with both the precision of a scientist and the sensuality of an epicure. "*Le vin est fait pour provoquer du plaisir*" ("Wine is made to give people pleasure"), he'd tell us in class almost every time we met. He'd then always quickly add that tasting wine *systematically* enables you "to measure just how much pleasure you derive from it—or don't."

Professor Peynaud's systematic approach to wine tasting involves assessing a person's experience of wine as seen through that person's eyes, nose, and, of course, tastebuds!

Visual Sensations: First, Drink In What You See!

Let's begin with what the eyes see. A wine's appearance is the first impression you have of that wine and is often an indication of its age, variety, and sometimes the region from which it comes. To get a good sense of a wine's true color, fill a wine glass so that it is approximately one-third full. Then tip the glass away from you until the wine approaches the inside rim. Look at the outer edge of the wine near the rim. Is the wine light, medium, or saturated in color? It's important to know that wine, being an organic (living) thing, is constantly changing its features as it grows older, and this includes its color. Young reds, for example, are purple, but they develop red orange and amber hues as they mature. In white wines, colors vary from a tinge of green to gold or even to amber as they age.

Judging Whites by Their Appearance

If you develop a disciplined eye, you'll be able to distinguish certain white wines by their color ranges. (A Pinot Gris, for example, is usually very light yellow, whereas a Chardonnay is a deeper yellow.) Meanwhile, white wines of all varieties also vary in color based on their age.

Table 7.1 will help you determine the age of a white wines.

TABLE 7.1   The Evolution of Color In White Wines

YOUNG	Green-tinged	Reflects youth, fullness
↓	Straw-colored	Majority of dry whites
	Gold	Usually represented by sweeter, more luscious wines
↓	Light brown	Indicates an older wine that may be off condition (although not always)
OLD	Brown/amber	Usually too old (suffering from excessive oxidation)

Note: If a white wine has been improperly stored (at too warm a temperature, for example) or has been exposed to air, its color will reflect this, showing a slight brown tinge or, worse, an amber tinge.

Judging Reds by Their Appearance

Reds aren't as obvious in their color changes as whites are. There are two dominant colors in red wine: red and (believe it or not) yellow. The red color comes from the pigmentation in the skins of purple grapes; the yellow color results from elements called tannins. Tannins exist in the skins, stems, and pits of grapes and enter the wine when the grapes are crushed. Some tannins also result when wine is aged in wooden barrels.

When a red wine is very young, its color tends to be purplish. Knowing this, you can tell when you are holding a young red wine in your hands. As a young wine matures, it loses some of that purple color to take on a purer red color. As it continues to mature, that red color begins to be lost and the color yellow becomes more evident, resulting in a red-orange color range. If a red wine takes on too much of an amber color, this is a sign that the wine is "overly mature" and should not be served. Table 7.2 will help you determine the age of red wines:

TABLE 7.2 The Evolution of Color In Red Wines

YOUNG	Purple	Young, immature wines
	Ruby red	No purple, indicating some age
↓	Red	Transition period; several years of age
	Red-brown	Mature wines
↓	Mahogany	Considerable maturity
OLD	Amber-brown	Very old or prematurely aged (oxidized); usually not to be served

Rose Wines

Rose wines should vary in range from pink to slightly orange. An amber color generally means the wine is too old.

One other thing about a wine's color: All wines should be clear and bright with no cloudiness evident. That said, some winemakers choose not to filter their wines, and these wines will show a certain haziness or cloudiness. Sometimes in white wine, there will be white crystals at the bottom of the bottle or on the cork. Don't worry about these; they are inert, tasteless tartrate crystals and are no cause for concern.

Olfactory Sensations: What the Nose Beholds

When it comes to wine appreciation, did you know that the nose really knows? Seriously, the human nose is 10,000 times more sensitive than our taste buds. Thus, it is an excellent lens through which to appreciate the nuances and fine points of a wine, especially its aroma or bouquet. In fact, 75 percent of the wine evaluation process can actually be accomplished with your nose alone, without the need to even taste the wine you're sniffing. But what fun would that be?

In human beings the olfactory organ is a small receptor deep in the back of the nose (see Figure 7.1). Consisting of nerve cells, this receptor is connected to nerve fibers along which smell impulses are transmitted to the brain. It is this small organ that determines whether you find a certain wine's scent to your liking or not.

Aroma and Bouquet

Sommeliers use two words to describe the smell of a wine: *aroma* and *bouquet*. Young wines usually have odors reminiscent of fruits or flowers: delicate, simple odors that reflect the grape from which they were harvested. They may also possess odors that result from the winemaking process (e.g., barrel aging). These odors constitute a wine's *aroma*. As a wine ages, it sheds its childhood qualities for a more developed, multidimensional, complex, and interesting odor. This we call *bouquet*. These scents are reminiscent of wood, vanilla, tobacco, tar, leather, earthiness, tea, and other things. *Aroma* is used to describe a wine in its youth; *bouquet* is used to describe a wine after it has matured to some degree. A wine does not possess aroma and bouquet at the same time.

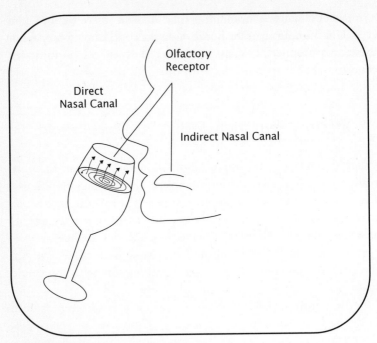

FIGURE 7.1 Retronasal Olfaction

The first thing to do in smelling a wine is to swirl the wine in a glass to concentrate the aroma or bouquet in the center. Next, bring your nose as close to the wine as possible. With the wine glass about one-third full, place your nose inside the glass, with your upper lip and nose touching the glass. Now, inhale deeply. By sniffing deeply, the strong intake of air forces the scent into contact with your olfactory receptor. Some wines have such a delicate fragrance that a normal sniffing will reveal almost nothing. After getting accustomed to sniffing deeply, however, you'll find it possible to detect distinctions between different wines and different grape varieties, even if the scent is very delicate.

Swirling wine in a glass (keeping the base of the glass on the table) and rotating it clockwise intensifies a wine's aroma or bouquet. Wine has alcohol in it, of course, and it's quite volatile. Alcohol acts as an aromatic support for the wine, so as a wine swirls, the alcohol evaporates out of the glass, bringing with it the particular scents trapped within.

Use the swirling and sniffing methods I've described here with every new wine you smell. Also, always put the same amount of wine in each glass that you use and never use different-sized glasses when comparing two wines, because both the quantity of wine served and the shape of the glassware used can impact a wine's aroma.

Once you start using your nose to effectively assess the aroma and quality of wine, a whole new world of wine appreciation will open up to you—I guarantee it! You'll begin to recognize wines by their characteristic scent. And as you grow in experience, you'll be able to discern and distinguish scents of raspberries, strawberries, melons, apples, prunes, and even bananas in the wines you taste.

Detecting Off Odors

As part of developing a nose for smelling wine, keep a couple of things in mind. First, a wine should smell like the variety of grape from which it is harvested. Repeated smelling and tasting sessions can enhance anybody's olfactory acuity in this area. Second, it's important for you, as a budding wine connoisseur, to be able to detect the "off odors" that can occur in a faulty bottle of wine. Whether you smell a simple, everyday table wine or a fine Château-bottled Bordeaux, it's important that there be no off odors. Off odors are usually produced when air leaks into the bottle, causing the wine to oxidize. The wine appears darker than usual, and its smell is reminiscent of sherry or Madeira. Such a wine, because of its odor, is said to be maderized. This can result from faulty corks, improper storage, or the wine being too old.

On occasion, when you open a bottle of wine you may also detect the smell of nail polish remover. All wines have some ethyl acetate in them (this is referred to as volatile acidity, or VA). However, when too much is present, it produces a harsh, unpleasant smell and the wine is defective. Sometimes, too, a sulfur smell is present in wines. Sulfur is used in most wines for its antioxidant properties, and it occasionally creates a slight burning sensation in the back of one's nose. Another off odor is corkiness. Corkiness results from a diseased cork, which, after a certain period of time, releases a very unpleasant smell (wet cardboard) that is unmistakable when it is encountered.

Taste Sensations: Now for the Really Fun Part

Obviously, as wine drinkers we live for the taste experience of wine. And with good reason! Did you know that your tongue (like your nose) is one of the most sophisticated sensory instruments known? It plays a critical role in helping discern and measure a wine's flavor. So, use it in tandem with your nose to maximize your wine tasting and appreciation experience. How can you do that?

Your tongue is covered with taste receptors, which we know, of course, as taste buds. If you were to look at a magnified version of your tongue (see Figure 7.2), you'd see that many of these taste buds appear to be in four distinct shapes, corresponding to the four elementary tastes that exist: sweetness, saltiness, sourness, and bitterness. It's worth noting that each of the four types of taste buds is receptive to only one of these basic tastes. A fifth taste, umami, which is sometimes described as "savoriness" or "deliciousness" and which is brought about by the interplay of glutamates and nucleotides (amino acids) in food and your mouth, is also at play and interacts with the other four tastes.

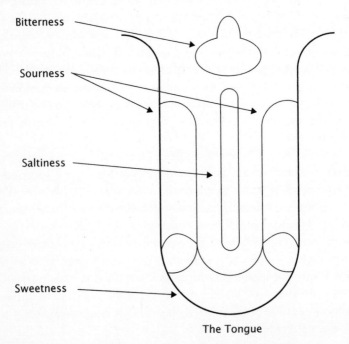

The Tongue

FIGURE 7.2   Elementary Flavors Overlap Each Other

Differentiating Tastes

How does your tongue actually differentiate among tastes? *Sweetness* is measured by the taste buds at the very tip of the tongue. *Sourness* is revealed by the taste buds along the sides of the tongue that also overlap with the sweetness taste buds at the tip of the tongue. *Saltiness* is measured by the buds concentrated in the center of the tongue and *bitterness* by those buds at the back of the tongue (see Figure 7.2). *Umami* is experienced through still other taste buds and is sometimes described as mouth filling or meaty. (For more on umami, visit the website of Tim Hanni, Master of Wine, sometimes described as the Swami of Umami. Tim has some radical views on balancing the flavors of food and wine. You'll find him at www.tim hanni.com.)

Obviously, it is hard for your taste buds to record all of these tastes simultaneously, so nature takes care of this for us. We experience sweetness first (again, those buds are at the tip of the tongue) before it dissipates. Next comes sourness and saltiness. When they fade, we taste bitterness. Umami is experienced as an overall sensation of the other four tastes working together and is sometimes described as a three-dimensional taste or flavor intensifier because of the impression it leaves in the mouth as a wine is drunk.

The *sweetness* of wine comes from natural grape sugars and the presence of alcohol. These elements play important roles in determining the overall sweetness of wines. Glycerine also contributes to the sweet taste, as well as to the mellowness of a wine. The *sour* taste, referred to by wine tasters as the acid taste, is a result of various organic acids. This is what gives "freshness" and "life" to wines. The taste of *saltiness* plays only a minor role in wines because its presence, due to mineral salts in the soil, is practically imperceptible. The *bitter* taste, resulting from compounds known as tannins, gives red wines both their skeletal structure and long life. Umami is a taste sensation stimulated by the presence of amino acids in food and saliva interacting with the other four tastes. It is experienced as helping bind and bring balance to the other tastes one is experiencing.

It's important that you understand this sequence of taste sensations, because this is why you must allow a wine to remain in your mouth long enough to give your tongue the necessary time to decipher all the aspects of flavor that the wine contains.

Other Factors That Affect the Taste of Wine

While we're on the topic of taste, let me mention a few other factors that can impact a person's wine tasting experience with a particular wine:

- *Body:* The term *body* refers to how a wine feels in your mouth or how it "fills" your mouth. When you describe a wine's feel in the mouth, you say it is *light bodied, medium bodied,* or *full bodied.* Light-bodied wines (think Pinot Grigio) are easy to drink. They go down as easily as water. Medium-bodied wines have more substance to them and seem to weigh more on the palate; they fill the mouth with a richer, more velvety quality. Full-bodied wines make their presence known in the mouth. They are assertive and can coat the tongue. A simple analogy is that light-bodied wines are like water; medium-bodied wines, like skim milk; and full-bodied wines, like rich, whole milk. Body is an important concept both in determining your own wine drinking preferences and in pairing specific wines with specific foods.

- *Sweetness range:* All wines contain sugar, alcohol, glycerine, acids, tannins, and so on. One speaks of a wine as being endowed with different amounts of these substances. The relative amounts of sugar and alcohol in a wine are what render it sweet, slightly sweet, or dry. The word *dry* implies an absence of sugar. Novice wine drinkers usually start out enjoying wines that are on the slightly sweet side. The more experienced wine drinker usually develops a taste for dry wines.

- *Flavor intensity:* Certain wines possess a greater flavor intensity than others. This can be due to any number of factors, including the grape varieties used and the winemaking techniques employed in the wine's production. Although people's tastes differ, it's important to recognize whether a wine is subtle and delicately flavored or, as with some intensely flavored reds, if it has a certain amount of bitterness. A person can learn these distinctions over time by sampling different kinds of wine. Flavor intensity can be thought of in terms of its concentration. For example, a full or intense flavor is analogous to the taste of a fruit juice concentrate before water is added to it. A delicate flavor is analogous to the way that concentrate tastes when water is added to it.

- *Time of tasting:* A person's ability to fully taste the distinctiveness of a wine is directly proportional to their degree of hunger when tasting it. For that reason, plan to serve samples of your best or most interesting wines at power entertaining events ahead of any food. This will help people focus on the quality of the wine or wines you are showcasing, before their appetites are dulled by eating too much.

- *The temperature of wines when served:* I've noted elsewhere that it's critical to serve wines at the appropriate temperature to optimize people's experiences of them. People in the United States generally serve red wines at too warm a temperature and white wines at too cold a temperature. The result is a diminished tasting experience in both cases! To prevent this, red wines should be tasted at a cool 65 to 68 degrees Fahrenheit. When reds are served above this temperature (as in most restaurants), they can be experienced as having a burning aftertaste due to the alcohol. Temperature also has an effect on your ability to evaluate a red wine's aromatics. If served too warm, the alcohol in a red wine becomes highly volatile and gives off an ethery odor.

  Like reds, white wines are equally affected by temperature. When served too cold (below 50 degrees Fahrenheit), the alcohol is inhibited from vaporizing and has trouble supporting the subtle aromatics that are present. Most white wines are served way too cold in restaurants because they are stored in very cold refrigerators where beer is also stored. You should always let white wines warm up a bit to fully appreciate their aromatics.

- *Glassware used:* When you serve wine at a power entertaining event, it's important that all wines be served in the same size glasses. The same wine tasted in a large glass will have a significantly stronger aroma than that same wine served in a small glass; this is because the alcohol volatilizes more quickly in a larger glass. For that reason, make sure all glassware at power entertaining events is of the same size and type. Also, samples to be tasted should be filled to the same level in glasses. A 2-ounce sample of a white burgundy is going to smell differently to people than a 3-ounce sample of the same wine.

Three Waves of Flavor

As noted, many people find it hard to describe the virtual cascade of tastes and sensations that occur in their mouths when they take a sip of wine. To remove that difficulty, let's talk more about Professor Peynaud's systematic approach to wine tasting that I mentioned earlier. Professor Peynaud's approach to wine tasting takes into account the time lag and the sequencing of tastes that somebody experiences when taking a sip of wine. Once you understand it, it will be easier for you to verbalize your impressions of how a wine tastes (see Figure 7.3).

When wine enters your mouth, it announces its presence as an initial impression. This is called a wine's *attack*. It's your first impression of the wine as it comes in contact with your tongue. Do you like what you taste? Or perhaps not? In any case, before you simply swallow the wine, wait to see if the wine's flavor and your impression of it evolves, perhaps developing more flavor intensity or richness. Professor Peynaud called this second stage of the tasting process the *evolution* of the wine's taste, because the flavor of the wine literally changes the longer it stays in contact with your taste buds. The evolution process reveals a wine's structure and complexity and takes anywhere from 1 second to 3 seconds, depending on the wine's quality and age. Last, comes something called the *finish* (aftertaste). This is the stage at which the wine has fully saturated your mouth with its final sensations (either positive or negative) and its presence has begun to decay. The finish can be experienced in different ways—as short, tart, and abrupt, or as lingering and tapering, coming to a quiet close or smooth end. Generally speaking, the longer a wine's aftertaste, the better the quality of the wine (and the more expensive its price)!

Table 7.3 shows precisely how the three steps of the tasting process work.

Want to give the taste of the wine you're drinking an extra kick? Do this: After you taste a wine and then swallow it, close your lips and immediately exhale the aromas in your mouth back through your nose. This will heighten your experience of the wine through a process the French call *retronasale* breathing.

TABLE 7.3 The Evolution of Flavor

ATTACK	You get your first impressions of a wine and perceive its degree of sweetness. (Duration: about 2 seconds.)
	↓
EVOLUTION	The wine's flavor expands and changes in your mouth. You perceive the wine's personality and complexity. Acidity and saltiness are also perceived. (Duration: 3 to 5 seconds)
	↓
FINISH	You develop a final impression of the wine as you swallow it. Confirmation of **ATTACK** and **EVOLUTION**. Bitterness is perceived. Simply put, the longer the aftertaste the better the wine!

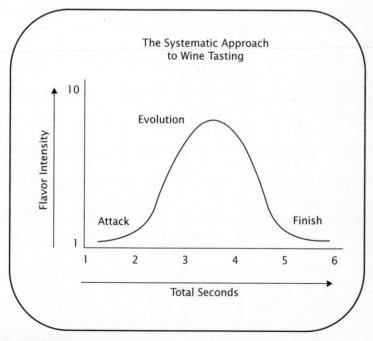

FIGURE 7.3 The Three Waves of Flavor in Wine Tasting

Finding Harmony and Balance in the Tasting of Wine

As I noted earlier, there are four primary tastes responsible for a wine's flavor: sweetness, acidity, bitterness, and umami. It is the subtle intermingling—the delightful dance and interplay of these elements in your mouth—that gives a wine its unique flavor signature and that creates a lasting impression!

To better understand why you might prefer one wine over another, you must first isolate the components responsible for a wine's flavor and then analyze the relationship among them. The amount of harmony between these components is what makes or breaks a wine. So let's talk about the notion of harmony in a wine because it's key to understanding a wine's character and quality.

Just as a symphony orchestra conductor strives to create a sense of balance and harmony among all the sections of an orchestra—the strings, brass, wind, and percussion elements—to produce pleasing results to the ear, a winemaker strives to balance the elements of sweetness, sourness (acidity), and bitterness in a wine. Sweetness is the only taste most people find agreeable; sourness and bitterness, by themselves, are relatively unpleasant. However, the winemaker attempts to create an excellent wine by blending in enough sweetness to counteract the sourness and bitterness also present in the wine.

All red wines for example, have some sourness (per the grape acidity) and bitterness (per the grape tannins), and without the neutralizing effect of sweetness (grape sugars/alcohol), they would taste sharp and biting. When these elements are in good balance, you have an excellent wine. In some years, if the grapes of a certain vineyard don't ripen due to lack of sunshine, they lack sufficient sweetness to balance out the acidity and tannins present. The result is an inharmonious wine, slightly sour, with a sharp finish.

Bottom line: in every glass of wine you sip, be it white or red, there's always going to be a tug-of-war going on between the elements shown in Figure 7.4.

Remember, wine is a chemical symphony of elements. Once you familiarize yourself with these elements, you'll recognize a good wine from a great wine with total comfort and confidence. To help

Sweetness → Acidity
← & Bitterness

It is precisely the amount of harmony between these elements that makes a wine of distinction.

FIGURE 7.4　A Tug-of War of Tastes

you with the harmonization process, take a look at Figure 7.5. This diagram displays the dynamics at work whenever you taste a red wine. It also provides a visual guide of things to consider as you taste a red wine to determine where your own taste preferences lie (e.g., sweet versus tart) and to assess how balanced or imbalanced you feel a wine is upon tasting it.

Your Palate Is as Unique to You as Your Fingerprints

This seems like a good point at which to mention something I think is absolutely essential to a fully satisfying experience of good wine, and it's this: although the notion of taste harmony and balance is important to understanding the structure and complexity of wine, it's really up to you to determine what kinds of wine you like and don't

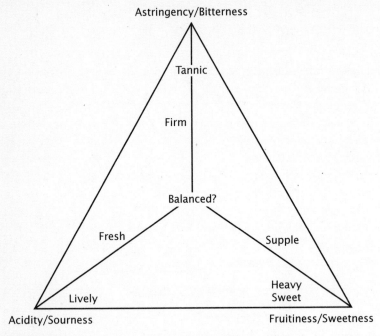

FIGURE 7.5   Finding Balance in the Flavor of Wine

like. That's because everybody's palate is unique; the combination of our taste buds and how they work together is specific to each and every one of us. Moreover, each of us has our own unique sensory awareness levels (thresholds of perception) to the tastes of sweetness, sourness, and bitterness. *For all these reasons, our palates are as unique to us as our fingerprints!*

Given this, it's really up to you to determine what you like, not for some wine critic to tell you what you *should* like! As Rajat Parr and Jordan Mackay note in their wonderful book, *Secrets of the Sommeliers*,

> Understanding your own palate is a matter of tasting lots of different wines and having confidence in your taste. It can be helpful to find critics or friends with palates you trust, but the final opinion must be your own.
> —Parr and Mackay, p. 72

How to Manage Paired Wine Samplings at Power Entertaining Events

Thus far in this chapter, I've talked extensively about the finer points of judging and tasting wine and as I learned to do at the l'Institut d'Oenologie, Bordeaux. To conclude this chapter, let's talk about how to actually introduce and conduct wine tastings at power entertaining events. In some cases, you'll be power pairing wines with food, as I discussed in Chapter 4. But in other instances, you may be doing a series of paired tastings of wine throughout an evening where the focus is primarily on the wine. In either situation, you have an opportunity at your events to educate people about the finer points of wine tasting and wine appreciation. This is a key component of power entertaining and part of what sets it apart from other, more traditional kinds of business entertaining.

Be Careful about Tasting and Buying

Sometimes you find unique wines that are never released to the public available for sale outside of wineries or vineyards you visit. Prices can be high; yet you may be tempted to buy something on impulse, especially if you just tasted it in the winery. Try to resist this!

I'll never forget the wisdom that Professor Peynaud shared with me and my classmates at the l'Institut d'Oenologie, Bordeaux, many years ago about impulse buying of wine. Knowing that many of us would become wine buyers or *négociants* (merchants or dealers) one day, he always told us, "Never make a significant purchase while tasting in the cellar! Ask instead that the château or winery send a bottle to your office so that you can taste it upon your return."

His words were crammed with wisdom. Wines do often seem to taste better when drunk in a cool, candlelit cellar, or when you are a bit high from an afternoon of wine tasting!

(continued)

(*continued*)

Professor Peynaud cautioned us that the atmospherics of a winery or vineyard or the psychology of certain situations can act as powerful "stimulus reinforcements" and warned us to beware of these, because they can cloud your palate's judgment of how a wine tastes.

So remember this the next time you visit a group of wineries some sunny afternoon and are tempted to buy a couple of cases of something that seems like the best wine you've ever tasted! It could be a very expensive proposition.

Instead, buy just one bottle. Or, better yet, ask the winery to send you a bottle of that wine to your home so you can judge (in the full light and sobriety of day) if you still want to order a whole case of it. You won't regret this!

So, what steps are actually involved in conducting a successful wine tasting? In Appendix F, you'll find a wine evaluation form that I recommend you print up and give to guests at your power entertaining events. This form is also downloadable at my website: www.eddieosterland.com. Use this form to let people conduct their own wine evaluations (and comparisons) of the wines you serve them at your event.

Here's the precise sequence of steps to follow:

Step 1: Ask guests to evaluate each wine's color and appearance. Remember, a wine's appearance is the first impression one gets of a wine and it can be an indicator of a wine's age, variety, and possibly the region or country it comes from. To get a good sense of the wine's true color, have your guests tip each glass of wine until the wine reaches the edge of the inside rim. Do this over a white tablecloth or piece of paper. Then have them look at the outer rim of the glass to determine the wine's true color. What do they see?

Step 2: Ask guests to evaluate each wine's "nose" (its aroma or bouquet). Instruct your guests on how to sniff a wine, as described earlier in this chapter. In each case, a wine's nose will range from nondistinct to very describable and/or intense. Tell your guests that the first whiff of a wine's aroma is critical. Subsequent whiffs tend to saturate a person's nose. So tell them to go with their first impressions! What adjectives would they use to describe the wine's aroma?

Step 3: Ask guests to evaluate each wine's flavor profile. They should begin by judging each wine's sweetness/fruitiness (its *attack*). This is the first impression a person perceives about a wine on tasting it, because the sweetness taste buds are located on the tip of the tongue. Wines from great vintages possess concentrated fruitiness resulting from ample sunlight, which fully ripens the grapes. Wines from lesser years (insufficient sunlight) have less intense degrees of fruitiness. The sweetness component of a wine is very important because it is needed to balance the sour elements (acidity) and bitter overtones (tannins) that are also present.

Step 4: Next, have guests evaluate how the wine's flavor evolves in their mouth. Remember, this is known as a wine's *evolution*. It takes anywhere from 2 to 5 seconds for a wine's flavor to fully evolve in a person's mouth. As it does, people can judge whether its sweetness and sourness come into balance in a way they like or not. Acidity drives the midpalate of a wine and determines what people experience the longer the wine remains in their mouths. A wine's acidity will vary, based on the ripeness of the grapes that were used to make it and when they were picked. Wine with insufficient acidity is referred to as fat, flabby, or cloying. Such wine has no edge and may seem dull to the taste. Acidity gives a wine its edge and amplifies the flavors perceived in the attack. Wines with too much acidity (not enough sunlight during the vintage) are overly sharp and edgy.

Great wines have a more prolonged evolution, with more nuances and distinctions becoming apparent the longer the wine is in a person's mouth. Lesser wines have a shorter evolution. In general, wines with a longer evolution will be more expensive wines, as they are more complex and developed. By contrast, everyday table wines will exhibit very little, if any, evolution. They are mere beverage wines, not wines of distinction or note.

As you conduct your side-by-side taste pairings, see if your guests can determine which of the two wines in each pairing is the better and/or more expensive of the two.

Step 5: As guests ponder the evolution of the wine in their mouths, ask them to evaluate the degree of balance among sweetness, sourness, and bitterness they're experiencing. Remember, only great wines are perfectly balanced. (These are exceptional and always cost more. Just like great works of art!) Most wines are not perfectly balanced, and their prices reflect this. On the Wine Evaluation Form, your guests can indicate whether they believe a wine is balanced or not.

Step 6: As guests sample each wine, ask them to rate the over-all feel of each wine in their mouths to determine its *body/volume*. Wines can range from light bodied (like water) to medium bodied (skim milk) to full bodied (whole milk.) Alcohol plays a key role in contributing body to a wine. Higher alcohol levels give a fuller body. Wine enthusiasts swirl their red wines and watch what are known as the legs or tears. In other words, they watch to see how slowly the wine clings to the glass after swirling. The slower the tears or legs, the higher the alcohol will be. Fast tears or legs always indicate lower alcohol levels.

Step 7: Ask your guests to describe their fleeting sense of the wine they are tasting as they swallow it. Remember, this is called the *finish*. One sign of a really good wine is a lengthy *finish*. At the l'Institut d'Oenologie, Bordeaux, my classmates and I were given stopwatches to measure the flavor decay in terms of seconds. A good way to explain this to your guests is to say, "The longer the aftertaste/finish, the better the wine!"

Aging Potential versus Drinkability

There's one other factor to consider when doing side-by-side comparisons of wines: aging potential versus drinkability. Winemakers always face a choice: Do they make a wine for current consumption, or do they produce a wine to be aged to bring its flavor to peak? Wines made for daily consumption (like many restaurant Merlots) are easy to drink. They are fruit-forward and have little or no bitter tannins. You can drink these wines as a beverage, with or without food. Other wines—with more pronounced acidity and tannin—are designed to be aged for 5 to 10 years (or more). They have a marked astringency (puckeriness) if drunk too young and taste more balanced if allowed to age. With time, the tannic backbone of such wines begins to soften, allowing the fruitiness/sweetness component of the wine to present itself. The goal is to age these wines until they are just ready to drink.

As you conduct side-by-side tasting events, ask your guests to share what they think about the drinkability of each wine that you have them sample. Ask them if they think a certain wine is better drunk at this moment or would benefit from aging. Do they like the wine on its own, or do they think that the wine's taste demands that it be paired with a specific food item to create good food/wine synergy?

Although conducting paired wine tastings is fun, it can also be a bit complex. Your local sommelier or wine merchant can help you plan and conduct wine tastings. They will be able to walk guests through the experience of each wine they're tasting and help them understand what they are experiencing. Having a sommelier on hand will also take the stress off of you and enable you to enjoy your guests and the wine being served!

Chapter Wrap-Up

In this chapter I've provided an overview of how to taste and appreciate wine in all its character, complexity, and beauty. Obviously, there's much more I could say on this topic. Remember, wine tasting should be a fun, multisensory experience; you'll want to bring your eyes, nose, and taste buds to the process. You'll also want to bring your brain, because truly appreciating wine is both an intellectual and sensual experience, as this chapter has revealed.

For more on the art and science of wine tasting, you may want to pick up a copy of *The Taste of Wine: The Art and Science of Wine Appreciation*, second edition, by Emile Peynaud (Wiley, 1996).

Professor Peynaud is my former professor at l'Institut d'Oenologie, Bordeaux, and I owe him a great debt of gratitude, as I learned so much about the art and science of wine tasting from him.

Learn the nuances of wine tasting and appreciation for yourself, and it will be something you can teach others as well. I can't think of a nicer gift to give to a client or business colleague than a deeper and more nuanced knowledge of wine tasting and of the world of wine in general. Which is what this whole book is all about!

8

Out of the Kitchen Closet

Coming Out as a Foodie

*Great thoughts, great bonds, and great satisfaction grow out of these hours that
we spend with others, sharing food and wine. It can never happen in minutes.*
—David Rosengarten
Author of *Taste: One Palate's
Journey through the World's Greatest Dishes*

Okay, I admit it. While I'm a Master Sommelier who loves wine,
I'm also a major foodie who loves to prowl the Internet for the
best places to buy the best foods to pair with the best wines. I do it for
clients all the time when I custom design power entertaining events,
but I also do it for myself when I'm preparing to entertain friends and
family at home. Given my foodie focus, it's a miracle, I guess, that I'm
not as big as a small house! But believe it or not, I do believe in mod-
eration (most of the time), both when it comes to drinking and eating.

Food is *the* critical dance partner to wine at power entertaining
events. So, in this chapter I introduce you to some of my favorite online
gourmet food merchants. Many of these merchants stock unique and
hard-to-find foods that you can't buy in traditional brick-and-mortar

gourmet shops or high-end grocery stores. By serving these items at power entertaining events you'll impress your guests and give them a true, gourmet eating experience they'll long remember!

Although you can obviously visit the websites of these companies directly, by using my website, www.eddieosterland.com, as the portal to access these merchants, you'll be eligible for special discounts on many food items. (More about that later.)

First, here's a brief overview of some of my favorite online food merchants.

Eddie's Favorite Online Food Emporiums

Each of these online food purveyors offers scrumptious delights that you'll be hard-pressed to find even in traditional gourmet and specialty grocery stores.

Farm-2-Market (Seafood)

For fresh seafood, I can't think of a better online food purveyor than Farm-2-Market, a Web-based seafood market that provides you with extremely fresh seafood within 24 hours of your ordering it online. Farm-2-Market boasts that their business bypasses traditional intermediaries, wholesalers, and food brokers to bring you seafood that is custom harvested and then delivered to your door via FedEx. From Farm-2-Market you can order caviar, crab, crawfish, Maine lobster, mussels and clams, oysters, scallops, shrimp, and much more. And, if you want to know how best to prepare such seafood delights, Farm-2-Market's website also contains recipes for everything from pan-sautéed sea scallops and poached salmon to lobster bisque, Maryland she crab soup, crawfish and sausage Gumbo, Alaskan halibut cheeks, and more. Mmm!

Farm-2-Market's seafood quality is unmatched in my experience. Even in many gourmet food shops and high-end grocery stores, the seafood in stock is as much as a week or so old. Farm-2-Market works with local fishermen to bring you seafood that couldn't be any fresher unless you caught it yourself!

La Tienda: The Best of Spain

Looking to experience the best cuisine that Spain has to offer? Then I strongly suggest you check out La Tienda. This family-run company based in Williamsburg, Virginia, and Alicante, Spain, has been doing business online since 1996 and works with a network of artisanal and small family businesses in Spain to bring online customers the best of Spanish cuisine and other culinary products. On La Tienda's website you can browse and buy from an extensive online grocery store that features the finest in Spanish food, including *jamón ibérico de bellota* (Spanish acorn-fed ham), Ventresca tuna, and *mantecados* and *polvorones* (Spanish shortbreads).

My very favorite La Tienda food item is *jamón ibérico*. This scrumptious and very unusual ham (which I've mentioned in other chapters) is produced only in Spain and is made from a type of pig called *cerdo ibérico* or *pata negra*, which lives only on the Iberian Peninsula. These pigs, supposedly descended from an ancient species of roaming Mediterranean boar, are notable for their black hooves and ability to store great amounts of fat. This enables the ham from these pigs to be cured for very long periods of time, giving it an intensely sweet and complex flavor.

D'Artagnan Natural and Organic Meats (French Cuisine)

Like La Tienda, D'Artagnan is an online purveyor of gourmet foods, both to individual foodies and to upscale restaurants. The company's website offers a vast inventory of food products that includes game meats (rabbit, venison, and wild boar), gourmet poultry (goose, pheasant, duck, capon, guinea hen, and Scottish game birds), and pâté de foie gras, duck mousse, and terrines.

D'Artagnan is committed to natural and sustainable food production and has been on the forefront of the organic food movement in the United States. Besides its extensive online inventory of food items for sale, the D'Artagnan website also includes tasty and memorable recipes for dishes such as veal osso bucco, spice-infused duck tacos, Anasazi cowboy chili with buffalo and nopales (fleshy green leaves), cassoulet D'Artagnan, and black truffle ice cream, among other things!

Because of the perishability of its products, D'Artagnan ships all online orders in sealed insulated boxes via FedEx overnight. This site is a winner for last-minute food preparation needs!

Russ & Daughters (New York Deli Food)

Every now and then we all have a yen for a good New York bagel with lox, some New York cream cheese or maybe some German potato salad or a traditional kosher meal. So where do you go for the real thing? To the streets of New York City, of course.

Russ & Daughters is a New York City–based purveyor of smoked fish, caviar, and other specialty foods for all occasions. Founded in 1914 by a New York City pushcart operator, and considered one of America's last authentic "appetizing" stores, Russ & Daughters is renowned in New York as the go-to place for caviar, smoked/cured sturgeon, herring, cream cheese, bagels, and much more. It's a tradition that's been nurtured in part by the four generations of the Russ family who have continuously kept their hands on the helm of this gourmet food shop for nearly a century now.

Russ & Daughters has garnered praise from food critics and news organizations alike, from people like food and kitchen meisters Anthony Bourdain and Martha Stewart, and from news organizations such as the *New York Times*, *People*, *Vogue*, and National Public Radio, among others.

If you happen to live in New York, I heartily recommend an in-person visit to Russ & Daughters. But if you can't get to the Big Apple very easily, try shopping for Russ & Daughters food items online. The company sells wholesale to restaurants and also retail to individual shoppers. It offers a rich selection of food items you can buy for power entertaining functions or, for holidays and special occasions like Passover, Thanksgiving, Rosh Hashanah, Yom Kippur, Chanukah, Christmas, New Year's Eve, Valentine's Day, Mother's Day, and other occasions. When it comes to gourmet specialty foods, Russ & Daughters truly represents New York's finest!

Gilttaste

Speaking of online stores, still another one you have to check out is Gilttaste, an online food and wine magazine and marketing emporium featuring a delectable and tempting array of meats, sweets, wine, cheese, prepared foods, seafood, and classy cookware and bakeware. Here you'll also find daily news stories from the chatty worlds of food and wine, as well as recipes and opinions from chefs, wine experts, and food experts. You'll glean tips for selecting the best food and wine gifts, learn secrets to making unforgettable chilis and fire-roasted guacamole, find recipes for crown roast and oyster stuffing, and be instructed on how to fearlessly roast and eat whole fish.

Truth be told, this site is more than a food emporium and online food and wine magazine. It's actually a rich repository of food and wine "thought leadership," a kind of Oxford library of recipes and epicurean wisdom that you'll want to return to again and again and again. On one occasion, for example, when I visited the site, I wandered for more than a half-hour through a dazzling array of dessert recipes, all colorfully illustrated with beautiful and tempting photographs of the finished products. Yum! It proved to me that Gilttaste has one of the most photogenic foodie websites I've ever come across.

Where to Go for Information and Advice about Wine and Food

While new and fabulous foodie websites are appearing on the web nearly every day, so, too, are great sources of advice and information about entertaining with wine and food. Here are just a few sites you should know about.

Jancis Robinson www.jancisrobinson.com

No tour of wine and food websites is complete without stopping to visit the site of Jancis Robinson, Master of Wine (MW), a British wine critic, journalist, and writer. Whether you're a newcomer to the wine scene or an ardent wine lover looking to expand your knowledge of all things wine related, this is a great site to visit. Robinson has written literally a shelf of books about wine, including *Tasting Pleasure: Confessions of a Wine Lover* and *Jancis Robinson's Wine Tasting Workbook*. She also served as editor of the *Oxford Companion to Wine*, considered by many people to be the foremost wine encyclopedia in the world, and writes a weekly wine column for the *Financial Times*.

Robinson brings a unique blend of pedigree and intellect to her work in the wine field. Although her site includes private memberships, as do other websites I mention in this chapter, there's also a wealth of free information about wine, winemaking, vintages, wine regions, and wine history that anyone can access. You should definitely check this site out to deepen your wine knowledge and get ideas for power entertaining parties and dinners.

Epicurious.com

Many confirmed foodies already know about Epicurious.com. You'll find great recipes on this granddaddy of foodie websites, one of the very first to appear on the Web. Owned by Condé Nast, the site offers visitors a wealth of information on cooking, eating, drinking, and entertaining. Want to know the secrets for cooking with chocolate? They're here. Want to know how best to pair food with beer? There are ideas galore. Want to get tips for convection or induction cooking? Look no further. Epicurious.com covers these and hundreds of other culinary topics in a vast online network of articles, columns, links, and blogs.

You could literally spend days on this site, exploring every link and taking an ever-deeper dive into the worlds of cooking, drinking, gastronomy, and entertaining. For my money, I'd first scope out the site to get ideas for novelty food/wine pairings that you might want to offer at power entertaining events. For example, if you want to get guests at an event to think (eat) out of the box, how about creating food/wine pairings that involve foods from Egypt, India, the Philippines, and even Ethiopia? Alternatively, if you simply want a good recipe for an at-home family meal, Epicurious.com can help with that, too. I particularly like how Epicurious.com allows you to access recipes by specific cuisine, country, culture, and region.

WineSpectator.com

The *Wine Spectator* is a popular and quite venerable lifestyle magazine (it's been around since 1976) and website devoted to wine, wine appreciation, and wine culture. Although I like the magazine a lot, I find the website even richer as a repository of information and resources about wine, and I think you will, too. Go to the website and check out the online course catalog of courses you can take about wine appreciation and winemaking regions. Or browse through the various sections of the site that deal with collecting, wine ratings, travel to different winemaking regions, and much more. Read about how to design and build a wine cellar or test your current knowledge of wine by taking an online quiz. There's even an online expert of whom you can ask tough wine-related questions. This is a fun and substantial website that should definitely be part of your own epicurean fantasy tour.

Still other food-related sites you should visit include:

- Refined Palate (www.lizziee.wordpress.com), run by a great friend of mine and rabid foodie, Liz Haskell
- The Tasting Table (www.tastingtable.com), which describes itself as the free daily e-mail service for adventurous eaters everywhere
- Marvesta Shrimp Farms (www.marvesta.com), which promises online shoppers delivery of the freshest shrimp available within 24 hours
- Foodie sites for 20- and 30-somethings. There are loads of these on the Web; check them out (and various wine blogs, too) by visiting my site: www.eddieosterland.com

As noted, you can find all the food merchants mentioned in this chapter on the Web by yourself. But by going through my website (www.eddieosterland.com) to order specific food products from these sites, you'll be eligible for special online discounts. A real deal!

Plus, on my site I continually add to my list of preferred foodie websites (and update current foodie website URLs, as necessary).

So think of my website as a convenient, one-stop shopping portal through which to access all the foodie websites you'll ever need.

Bon appetit, mes amis!

9

Power Entertaining at Home

People live in different sensory worlds. We need to acknowledge that.
—Tim Hanni, MW

Throughout this book, I've talked about the principles of power entertaining and how to apply them in a business context. But did you know that you can also use power entertaining principles at home to entertain and impress family and friends?

To do this right, I strongly encourage you to start a personal wine collection and to use this collection as the basis for designing wine tastings and wine/food pairings that you can incorporate into private dinner parties, family gatherings, and other special events.

Wine collecting is a fabulous hobby. It can be tremendously absorbing, as many wine aficionados will confess, and it is an activity to which you can devote enormous amounts of time, dollars, and interest, if you wish. But starting a personal wine collection doesn't have to be difficult, expensive, or time-consuming. In fact, you can start a great home wine collection with just 50 or so bottles of wine that are ready, at any time, for service to family and friends.

Start by building an initial home inventory of wines that enables you to serve interesting themed pairings to close friends and family members. Next, I share my three favorite themes for home-based power entertaining events and some of the wines to buy for service to family and friends.

Themes for Power Entertaining at Home

Theme #1: New World versus Old World

You know by now that this is one of my favorite themes when doing side-by-side wine comparisons at business-related power entertaining events. So why not do this same themed wine pairing at home with friends and family? If this theme appeals to you, here are some good New World and Old World wines to stock in your home inventory for future dinner parties:

- Sauvignon Blancs from New Zealand, France, and California
- California Cabernet versus French Bordeaux
- California Chardonnay versus white burgundy
- California Pinot Noir versus French burgundy versus Oregon Pinot Noir

Minimum number of bottles required for this tasting: 10

Be sure to buy enough bottles of each wine to accommodate whatever number of guests you want to have taste these wines in tandem. Plan on getting eight 3-ounce servings per bottle or six 4-ounce servings per bottle. In any case, you don't want to run out of stock at your party, so buy 10 percent more stock than you think you'll need.

Theme #2: Introducing Different Wines of the World

Another way to introduce guests to different wines is to expose them to wines of different wine-producing regions. This can be loads of fun and quite educational. Doing regionally focused tastings helps people learn about and appreciate the *terroir* of different wines and how wines of the same vintage (year) can differ from one another based on where they are produced. (You'll recall that the term *terroir* refers to the characteristics of the locale, climate, geography, and soil in which a particular wine is produced. It is the combination of these factors in any given year that gives a wine its unique personality and taste—its flavor signature.)

There are infinite ways to compare and contrast wines by region, but here are some surefire lineups that your guests will enjoy and that will keep them talking about your event for days afterward. Think of doing one or more of these regional pairings at a home gathering, depending on the amount of time you have (an entire evening or an afternoon) and the interests of those attending:

- Beaujolais (compare and contrast Beaujolais—Villages and Cru Beaujolais)
- Pacific Northwest wines (compare and contrast Oregon Pinots, Washington Cabernets and Merlots)
- Germany (compare and contrast dry German Rieslings and fruity-style Rieslings)
- France (compare and contrast Bordeaux and burgundy)
- Italy (compare and contrast the "three Bs of Northern Italy"— Barolo, Barbaresco, and Barbara)
- Italian whites (compare and contrast Gavi and Arneis)
- Chablis styles (compare and contrast Petite, Premier Cru, and Grand Cru)
- Spanish whites (compare and contrast Albariño and Godello)
- Spanish reds (compare and contrast Rioja reds [Crianza and Gran Reserva])
- Alsace (compare and contrast Riesling, dry Muscat, Pinot Gris, Gewürztraminer)
- Rhône (compare and contrast Côtes du Rhône and Gigondas or Saint- Joseph)
- Minimum number of bottles required for this tasting: 27

My hunch is that after exposing people to the side-by-side tastings I've suggested, they will shower you with thanks for pushing them beyond their normal comfort zone of garden variety Chardonnays, Merlots, and Cabernets!

Theme #3: Battle of the Bubblies

You know that I have a sweet spot in my heart for sparkling wines, so in my view, no home wine tasting is complete without including bubblies in the festivities. If you decide to do paired wine tastings at home with bubbles, here are my suggestions of what to pair. Try:

- Cava versus Prosecco versus Sekt versus Crémant d'Alsace
- French champagne (nonvintage versus vintage grower)
- California sparklers (blanc de noirs, brut blanc de blanc)

Minimum number of bottles required for this tasting: 8

There you have it! Just three potential themes for wine tastings that you can conduct at home, but of course there are many, many more! Notice that if you bought just one bottle of each of the wines I describe in the three themed tastings, you'd immediately have a collection of 45 bottles, which is enough to impress anybody.

Best Wines for Home Entertaining $40 and Under

James Tidwell, Beverage Manager and Master Sommelier, Four Seasons Resort and Club Dallas at Las Colinas, recommends the following.

Whites

"Assyrtiko from the Greek island of Santorini makes a choice for those who want to try a crisp, minerally white wine. Italian white wines such as Roero Arneis, Greco, and Falanghina are hits with many people as well. South American wines from grapes such as Semillon and Viognier offer richer flavor profiles for those who enjoy more weight. And, of course, Texas wines, since I work in the state; Viognier and Roussanne are particular favorites from Texas!"

(*continued*)

(*continued*)

Reds

"Cabernet Franc in all its guises works as a familiar, yet different, variety. Less expensive Douro blends satisfy those looking for mineral and fruit. Old Vines Carignan from Chile has the richness to complement beef, an important quality for wine in Texas. Texas does a great job with lesser known red varieties such as Touriga and Tannat, although Tempranillo and Sangiovese are some of the best red varieties currently in Texas. Most are inexpensive."

And here's an idea for you: Before your next home dinner party, why not fill your wine refrigerator or cooler with wines reflective of *all* three of these themes and make up a wine list of your inventory? Then give your guests the list of themes and ask them to pick those wines to drink that they'd most like to learn about. Not only will this get people to engage with one another, it's also a very generous gesture on your part. Most people serve their guests only what they like to drink, not what their guests might enjoy having!

Storing Wines for Home Use

"Okay, Eddie," you ask, "how do I best store my wines for home use?"

This is a great question to ask, and obviously one you must address to build a home inventory of wines for service to family and friends. First, forget about keeping your wines in one of those small metal or wooden wine racks on the top of your kitchen counter or refrigerator. Between seasonal changes in light and temperature and the vibrations of people coming and going through your house, the kitchen is a lousy place to store wine unless you want to accelerate its decline into vinegar. Ugh! And although you could build yourself a home-based wine cellar, doing so can be expensive and requires careful attention to many details of design, temperature, and location.

Best Wines for Home Entertaining $40 and Under

Brandon Tebbe, MS, CWE, CSS, Director of Wine, Beverage & Restaurant, Paulée Dundee, Oregon, recommends the following.

Whites

- Monastero Suore Cistercensi "Coenobium" 2009, Lazio, Italy (retails for about $30)
- Lopez de Heredia "Vina Gravonia" Crianza 2002, La Rioja, Spain (retails for about $25)

Rose

- Lucien Albrecht, Crémant d'Alsace Brut Rosé N.V. (retails for about $22)

Reds

- Kalin Cellars "Cuvée DD" Pinot Noir 1999, Sonoma County, California (retails for about $40)
- Knipser "Blauer Spatburgunder" Trocken 2008, Pfalz, Germany (retails for about $30)
- Infinite Money Theorem Malbec 2010, Grand Valley, Colorado (retails for about $28.99)
- Investing in a Wine Cooler or Refrigerator

As an alternative to both these ideas, I recommend you first invest in a small, under-the-counter or free-standing wine storage cooler or refrigerator, one that can hold 40 to 50 wine bottles quite easily. A wine storage cooler/refrigerator isn't a wine cellar; instead, it is a holding unit designed for short-term wine storage, usually less than a year. Such units can store a nice selection of wines, ready to drink at any time.

One major benefit of owning a wine refrigerator/cooler is that it gives you a dedicated, climate-controlled space away from your food refrigerator to store both white and red wines at their appropriate temperatures. A wine cooler/refrigerator is one of the most important "power tools" any power entertainer can own! I own two coolers, one of which I keep at 48 degrees for whites and the other at 58 degrees for reds. (*Note:* 58 degrees is a bit too cold for reds but, after opening them up and decanting them, they will warm to about 65 degrees by the time you serve them, which is the perfect temperature!)

Besides wine refrigerators and coolers, another way to store wine is in a temperature-controlled wine cabinet designed for long-term storage that you can easily keep in your garage.

Choosing the Right Wine Cooler or Cabinet

When shopping for either wine coolers/refrigerators or cabinets, here are some things to keep in mind:

- *Buy a unit that will reliably protect your wines from heat, light, and vibration.* Storing wines at too warm a temperature causes them to prematurely age. Vibration has the same effect, and light damages wines as well. For all these reasons, the wine refrigerator or cabinet you buy should have a robust and reliable cooling system (to maintain temperatures at between 55 and 58 degrees). It should have opaque doors to screen out UV light. And it should operate quietly to control or minimize vibrations.

- *Determine what size unit you need.* Wine cooling refrigerators come in many different sizes and price ranges, from as low as $90 to as pricey as $4,000! My very favorite brand is Sub-Zero, a company that produces units of various capacities. I own the Sub-Zero 424, which holds 46 bottles. One of the things I like about this unit is that it has dual compressors, which allows me to set the two compartments of the unit at different temperatures for whites and reds.

- *If you're on a tight budget, buy a wine cooler that has only one temperature range and use it for your reds.* You can keep your whites in the fridge and just remember to take them out 20 minutes before service.

- *Proper humidity settings are critical to proper wine storage.* For both reds and whites, the humidity setting in the unit should be set at between 55 and 75 percent. Below this temperature, corks begin to dry out, and above it, both corks and labels can become moldy and disintegrate.
- *Buy a unit with good racking.* Cheap units often have flimsy wine racks.

Best Wines for Home Entertaining $40 and Under

Richard Dean, Master Sommelier, The Taj Campton Place in San Francisco, California, recommends the following.

White

- Riesling Kabinett Zilliken "Saarburger Rausch" Mosel 2009

Red

- Rioja La Montesa Palacios Crianza 2007

Makers of High-Quality Wine Refrigerators

As already noted, I'm a big fan of Sub-Zero wine refrigerators. Not only are these wonderful appliances, they also make great kitchen art that can last a lifetime! That said, there are other brands of refrigerators you may want to consider. *Consumer Reports* has done extensive research on wine refrigerators and gives very high marks to the Kenmore 9913 ($500). You can buy it at Sears, and it holds 38 bottles. Another brand to consider is the Marvel 6SWC ($1,500), which holds 54 bottles. *Consumer Reports* also gives a high rating to the GE wine cellar ($1,200). Still another brand to consider is Haier, which makes a 35-bottle dual-zone unit, available at Walmart ($399), which holds just 12 bottles of wine and sells for $100. (Despite this low price, the unit comes with double-paned insulated glass doors, an adjustable thermostat, and chrome shelves.)

Now that I've given you tips about what to look for in a wine refrigerator/cooler, it's time for you to pick a brand and model that are best for you. To help you do this, visit the website of the Wine Cooler Expert at www.winecoolerexpert.com. This site contains a wealth of information on wine refrigeration units and what to consider in buying units for home entertaining. You'll see information on every major brand and model of wine cooler on the market today, and you'll be able to do some informed comparison shopping to see what most appeals to you. Here's the specific link on the Wine Cooler Expert site to go to: www.winecoolerexpert.com/40-50-bottle-wine-coolers.html.

Other Storage Options: Wine Lockers

Thus far in this chapter, I've emphasized wine coolers/refrigerators as the way to go, especially if you are a newbie to wine collecting. But your goals, even from the start, may be more ambitious. If this is the case, you may want to rent a wine locker at one of the many wine storage facilities in your area. Wines can be stored properly in such lockers for as little as $1 per bottle per year, but make sure the locker company you choose has been in business a long time, is secure, and has proper insurance. I believe in wine lockers because they are a great place to house wines you own that need at least 7 to 10 years of aging to reach maturity. They're especially good for housing fine Bordeaux, burgundy, and Barolo wines, among others. Renting space for your wines away from home means you won't be tempted to drink them before they reach maturity. And if you add new wines to this off-site wine locker each year, eventually you'll start to have high-quality mature wines that you can uncork each year for service to friends and family at home.

Best Wines for Home Entertaining
$40 and Under

Dustin Wilson, Master Sommelier and Wine Director, Eleven Madison Park, New York City, recommends the following.

Whites and Reds

When guests want something different, especially at a lower price point, I find that indigenous varieties from Old World countries and wines from lesser known appellations are a gold mine. Grapes like Schiava from Alto Adige or Blaufränkisch from Austria are really delicious wines that offer incredible value. This, of course, is just the tip of the iceberg. There are thousands of options out there. In these situations, I try to avoid a classic or "international" grape from a well-known region. You just can't get great Napa Valley Cabernet in a restaurant for $40. So have fun with quirky wines instead!

So You Want to Build a Wine Cellar?

Okay, I admit, after buying a wine refrigerator or a wine cabinet, you may quickly discover that your love of wine collecting continues to grow and knows no limits. This happens! Why? Part of the reason is that the more you learn about wine, the more diverse your taste becomes. A second reason is that once you find things you like, there's a tendency to want to buy these items to share with others. This is where the real joy of collecting wine and entertaining with wine comes fully into play. In my experience, most people don't collect wines to drink by themselves; the fun is in sharing them with others!

Considerations When Building a Cellar

When your house begins to overflow with wine bottles, it's time to consider building a bona fide wine cellar! If you're going to build a wine cellar, remember that the three things you must tightly control are:

1. Temperature (maintained at a constant 55 degrees Fahrenheit)
2. Humidity (65 percent is recommended)
3. Light (which needs to be limited)

Wines, especially reds (which will make up the majority of your collection), need to age at a constant temperature to properly mature. Wherever you store them, you must control the ambient temperature to avoid extremes. As noted earlier, by keeping the humidity constant you protect corks from drying out and labels from getting moldy. Light must be controlled as well. This is why most wine bottles are green or brown—to keep light out.

When You Care to Have the Very Best

Okay, so you've decided to go all the way and build a wine cellar in your home. Great! If that's the case, knowledge, experience, and craftsmanship will be key to building a wine cellar of lasting enjoyment that will be the repository of the cherished wines you carefully add to your collection through the years.

When it comes to building high-end custom wine cellars, two premium vendors I recommend you consider using are Revel Custom Wine Cellars and the Magnum Company. Both companies pride themselves on their unique craftsmanship in building high-end wine cellars for clients. And, in my experience, both bring novel and even breakthrough thinking to their concepts of wine cellar design and wine cellaring. For more information on each, visit my website: www.eddieosterland.com.

Building a wine cellar at home requires you to consider issues of space and budget. To keep costs down you may want to think about converting a closet or a spare room of your house into a cellar. If you do this, all you need to do is properly insulate the space from light and vibration and install a temperature/humidity unit. There are many online contractors you can contact for quotes to do such work. Make sure you work with companies that specialize in wine cellar design. (Do *not* use a general contractor.)

Following are a few online providers to consider getting quotes from:

www.apexwinecellars.com

www.artisticcellars.com

www.iwawine.com

www.vintagecellars.com

www.westsidewinecellars.com

Best Wines for Home Entertaining $40 and Under

Roger Dagorn, Master Sommelier and Wine Director, Porter House New York, New York City, recommends the following.

Whites

- "Sainte Claire" Chablis, Jean-Marc Brocard 2008 ($39)
- Etude Pinot Gris, Napa 2010 ($39)

Reds

- Ruca Malen Petit Verdot, Mendoza, Argentina 2009 ($30)
- Albertina Reserve Cabernet Sauvignon, Mendocino, California 2005 ($30)

Stocking Your Wine Cooler or Wine Cellar

Wine cellars are for storing "better" and "best" wines, wines that usually cost at least $25 to $35 a bottle when released. When it comes to stocking a cellar, don't make the mistake of collecting only California wines. There are so many great wine-growing regions out there today that you'll want to have a good representative sampling of wines from many regions. Here are just some of the most famous wines that you should think about cellaring.

Whites

- German, Austrian, and Alsatian Rieslings (they age easily for 20 to 30 years)
- French white burgundies (Chardonnays)
- California Chardonnays (expensive ones)
- Dessert wines from Germany, France, Italy, Portugal, and the United States (remarkable age worthiness)

Reds

- French: Bordeaux, burgundies, and Rhône Valley wines
- Spanish: Rioja, Ribera del Duero
- Italy: Piedmont (Barolo, Barbaresco), Tuscany (Chianti Classico Riserva, Super Tuscans, Brunello di Montalcino)
- California: top Cabernets and Pinot Noirs, Syrah, and Zinfandel
- Australia: Shiraz and Cabernet Sauvignon, blends

Other Considerations When Power Entertaining at Home

When power entertaining at home, it's not enough simply to have enough red and white wine on hand. Consider also what beers you may want to offer people (see Chapter 6). I also recommend that you have a small selection of predinner apéritifs and postdinner digestifs on hand to serve to guests. Among my favorites are:

- Lillet Blanc, a wonderful apéritif (before-dinner drink) from Bordeaux that has aromas of apricots, peaches, and oranges. Serve it to people over ice with a flamed orange peel. People often love this!
- Carpano Sweet Vermouth, which is rich, viscous, and loaded with botanical flavors of herbs, plum, spice, almonds,

---

and bitter marmalade. Pour it over ice with a twist, or use it to glaze a scoop of vanilla ice cream. Yum!

- Amaro Montenegro, a digestif (after-dinner drink) from Italy. This is one of a family of drinks called bitters. If you stock only one, Amaro Montenegro should be it! It has botanical accents of orange peel, fresh coriander, cherry, pekoe tea, and cucumber finishing with bitter tangerine overtones.

What kinds of nonalcoholic beverages should you have on hand? Two drinks I like to serve guests are Vichy Catalan, a wonderful and robust sparkling water from Spain that you hardly ever see anywhere. Also, consider sodas made by the Seattle-based Dry Soda Company. This is truly soda for grown-ups! It's absolutely delicious without the over-the-top sweetness of virtually every traditional soda on the market today. Dry Soda Company makes sodas in seven distinct (and low-cal) flavors, including Wild Lime, Lavender, Blood Orange, Rhubarb, Juniper Berry, Vanilla Bean (my favorite), and Cucumber. These are incredibly refreshing and a treat for anyone to experience!

Chapter Wrap-Up

This chapter has focused on things you can do to take your home entertaining to a whole new level. That process begins with the building of a diverse home inventory of wines that you can use to support your home entertaining activities. Besides being a lot of fun, building a home wine inventory has a lot of benefits. Not only can it help you plan enjoyable and memorable power entertaining events for friends and family at home, it can also help you grow in your knowledge and appreciation of wines. You'll learn what you enjoy as you build your home collection. And you'll learn about the many distinctions and nuances among wines as you design wine pairings to share with family and friends.

After you've had the experience of buying and using a wine refrigerator or cooler for a while, you may decide to take the next step—to store vintage wines for aging in a wine storage facility away from your house or to build a wine cellar in your home.

But before you do either of these things, cut your teeth on power entertaining at home by first buying a nice wine cooler or refrigerator. You may find it's all you really need to bring a whole new dimension to your home entertaining.

10

Masterminds

From Wine Geek to Wine Expert

Attempting, much less passing, the Master Sommelier Examination is as thorough a test of specific skills as one can imagine. One might believe that single factors such as talent, mentorship, technology or a combination would create success. It is my opinion that the time honored fundamentals of professionalism, dedication and HARD WORK continue to be the deciding factors in those achieving the Master Sommelier Diploma.

—Fred Dame
MS, President, Guild of Sommeliers

I f you've read this far in this book, I suspect that you're more than a mere fan of wine; you're probably a real aficionado—even a wine geek—who lives and breathes wine nearly as much as I do. If that's the case, you might want to consider taking your love and knowledge of wine to an even deeper level by acquiring a professional wine credential. Doing so could prove a wonderful educational opportunity for you to learn more about a subject for which you have already professed a deep love.

With that in mind, this chapter talks briefly about some of the principal wine credentials out there that you may want to consider pursuing. Acquiring one or more of these credentials could potentially launch you on a career path as a sommelier, wine merchant, wine educator, or wine critic, writer, or vintner.

What Is It with All Those Initials?

If you've spent any time in the company of sommeliers and wine merchants, you've no doubt noticed the confusing jumble of letters that often come after the names of people considered experts and gurus in the world of wine. Those initials include MS, which stands for Master Sommelier (a designation I hold); MW, which stands for Master of Wine; CSW, which stands for Certified Specialist of Wine; and DWS, which stands for Diploma in Wines and Spirits. There are still other initials that people can collect and put after their names, and this chapter talks briefly about what each credential means and the course of study typically involved in acquiring each.

In the world of wine today, the two most prestigious distinctions one can acquire are those of Master Sommelier and Master of Wine.

Master Sommelier

The designation of Master Sommelier (MS) is the most prestigious credential awarded by the Court of Master Sommeliers, an international organization founded in 1977 that is committed to promoting excellence in hotel and restaurant beverage service around the world. The MS distinction is awarded to professionals in the hospitality and beverage service industries who successfully complete all four levels of a rigorous wine education program. On the way to achieving the MS distinction, an individual must first complete an introductory wine course and exam, followed by further study and an examination that, if passed by an individual, leads to recognition as a Certified Sommelier (CS). Further study and examination then follow and can lead to recognition as an Advanced Sommelier (AS). After yet more preparation and study, an individual may be invited to sit for the Master Sommelier Diploma. To date, fewer than 200 people have been awarded the MS designation worldwide.

Besides emphasizing the study and production of wine, the CS, AS, and MS diplomas also emphasize rigorous training and mastery of the business sides of the beverage service industry. This includes developing expertise in beverage department management, restaurant/customer service, wine tasting/pairing, and wine knowledge/production. In completing any of these diploma programs, an individual is also expected to be knowledgeable about spirits, beers, and cigars.

You might think that acquiring any of these credentials would be a cakewalk for somebody who already loves wine, but that's not the case. Indeed, the jump from wine hobbyist to wine professional is a big leap! Acquiring any of these distinctions involves a lot of hard work, study, and meticulous preparation for a career in the beverage or hospitality industry—most likely in a restaurant, resort, or some other demanding, fast-paced retail service environment. For more information on any of the Court of Master Sommelier designations you can acquire, follow the links below.

Introductory Course and Exam

www.mastersommeliers.org/Pages.aspx/Introductory-Sommelier-Course

Certified Sommelier

www.mastersommeliers.org/Pages.aspx/Certified-Sommelier-Exam

Advanced Sommelier

www.mastersommeliers.org/Pages.aspx/Adv-Sommelier-Course-and-Exam

Master Sommelier

http://mastersommeliers.org/Pages.aspx/Master-Sommelier-Diploma-Exam

Master of Wine

The Master of Wine (MW) designation is awarded by the Institute of Masters of Wine, a London-based organization that promotes professionalism, excellence, and "knowledge of the art, science and business of wine." Although the CS, AS, and MS designations are normally conferred on individuals working in the beverage and hospitality industries, the MW designation is a more academic credential that involves deep scholarly study of wine, grape growing, production techniques, and the science of grape maturation. Holders of this designation also must complete rigorous research and writing requirements to secure the MW distinction. The MW is a professional credential often pursued by wine writers, critics, merchants, and producers. This credential does not focus on preparing wine professionals for work in a retail service setting, such as a restaurant.

Passing the MW exam is a grueling process that often takes as long as five years to complete. Written exams are given once a year. Candidates for the MW distinction must also complete a 10,000-word dissertation. An individual is eligible for membership in the Institute of Masters of Wine after they have successfully passed the exam and completed the course of studies.

Society of Wine Educators

If you don't see yourself actually working in a retail service environment or becoming a wine "scholar," critic, or writer, there are still other professional designations that might be of interest to you. The goal of the Society of Wine Educators (SWE) is to promote professional education among wine professionals and to increase professionalism within the wine industry as a whole. SWE offers three certification programs that are highly regarded in the wine and spirits industries. The programs award the designations Certified Specialist of Wine (CSW), Certified Specialist of Spirits (CSS), and Certified Wine Educator (CWE). A person with any of these credentials next to their name has formally displayed a deep knowledge of wine and the ability to teach and communicate to others about it. Acquisition of any of these credentials is often a preliminary step toward pursuing the designation of Master Sommelier or Master of Wine. For more information on SWE programs, go to www.societyofwineeducators.org.

French Wine Scholar

The French Wine Scholar (FWS) is a wine study and certification program offered by the French Wine Society. Acquiring the FWS designation signals that an individual has developed a deep knowledge of various French wine regions. Thus, one can be designated as a Bordeaux Master, a Rhône Master, a Provence Master, and so on. Classes and certification programs are offered online, and some courses are also taught in classrooms in France. The beauty of FWS's programs is that they approach the study of wine from a uniquely French perspective, as opposed to an American or British perspective, which is typical of the MS and MW distinctions, respectively. For more information on FWS courses and programs, visit www .frenchwinesociety.org.

The Wine & Spirits Education Trust

The Wine & Spirits Education Trust (WSET) is an organization that offers wine courses, certificates, and diplomas designed to prepare individuals for pursuit of the MS or MW credential. The highest-level distinction WSET offers is the Diploma in Wines and Spirits, or DWS. Completion of the DWS program is a significant professional achievement and demonstrates a strong commitment to the study of both wine and spirits. Check out the WSET website at www .wsetglobal.com.

The International Sommelier Guild

The International Sommelier Guild (ISG) is yet another organization that certifies professional sommeliers. It provides students with access to leading restaurateurs, wine merchants, and wine educators, and it has the distinction of offering wine courses and a six-month sommelier diploma program in Chinese. ISG, in fact, is doing a great deal of work with wine professionals today in China. ISG also offers sommelier classes and diplomas in the United States and Canada. You can learn more about ISG programs by visiting the ISG website at www.internationalsommelier.com.

The Guild of Sommeliers

Still another organization to check out is the Guild of Sommeliers (www.guildsomm.com), a nonprofit membership organization made up of 3,500 sommeliers, wine merchants, wine enthusiasts, and others. Although it does not confer formal credentials, it has an extensive website on everything related to wine and is dedicated to promoting education, development, communication, and collaboration among wine professionals in all aspects of the food and beverage and hospitality industries.

As Geoff Kruth, MS, and Chief Operating Officer of the Guild, puts it: "The Guild is very much dedicated to the ongoing professional development of its members because our industry is constantly changing. Today there are literally thousands of wine regions and thousands of wine grapes with which sommeliers need to be familiar. What's more, laws regarding wine production are constantly changing the world over. For these and many other reasons, the Guild offers members a wide variety of educational and professional development opportunities focused on wine knowledge, wine regions, geography, and the law. Formats for training range from online discussions to networking opportunities, enrichment programs, scholarships, and more."

Other Organizations of Interest

Finally, two other organizations you may also want to check out are the American Sommelier Association (ASA), at www.americansom melier.com, and the United States Sommelier Association, at www .ussommelier.com.

Chapter Wrap-Up

Although this chapter has showcased some of the major credentials one can acquire as a wine professional, and some of the major professional organizations to which wine professionals belong, it bears saying that there are many fine and highly competent sommeliers working in the beverage and hospitality industries today who possess no formal credentials at all. Yet, through their dedication, professionalism, service, and commitment to professional growth on the job, they have distinguished themselves as wine professionals of the highest order. Working in leading restaurants, resorts, and other venues around the world, they clearly demonstrate both professional integrity and excellence in the work they do, be it in restaurants, resorts, corporate settings, colleges and universities, professional wine organizations, or elsewhere.

Epilogue

Taste Life Now!

Okay, my friend, you've now reached the end of my book. In these pages I've tried to share all I know about how to entertain others, using good wine and food as the currency for bringing people together and creating memorable moments that people will remember for a long, long time. As my 98-year-old father used to say, "Eddie, life is really nothing but a set of special moments that we look back on fondly throughout the course of our lives."

I couldn't agree with him more! By embracing the principles of power entertaining outlined in this book, you'll be able to create special moments for others, be it in business settings with colleagues and clients or in your own kitchen, dining room, or living room with the people in your life who matter most—your family and friends.

As I wrap up, I want to share just a couple of closing thoughts about power entertaining and why I do what I do as a sommelier. . . .

Power entertaining isn't just about good wine and good food. It's about PEOPLE and helping PEOPLE connect with one another. In my role as a host and sommelier, I love to connect people with one another in situations that can be to everyone's mutual benefit. In that sense, I like to think of myself as being what Malcolm Gladwell, author of *The Tipping Point*, would call a "connector," somebody who enjoys introducing people to others and helping others build strong and vibrant social and professional networks. In this book it's been my goal to help *you* become a connector as well, someone who can open doors to and for others and who will reap great rewards (both personal and professional) from doing so.

Second, power entertaining is about giving to others and receiving back the joys of friendship, collegiality, and appreciation that flow from extending generosity and hospitality to others. In this world I really believe that what goes around comes around. A quick story will describe what I'm talking about here. About five years ago I did a corporate retreat in Denver for 50 executives of a large international company. As part of the wine tasting, I bought several cases of 1996 Château Pichon-Lalande, a luscious and very expensive Bordeaux for people to sample. At the end of the event, I had a $500 magnum of this magnificent wine left over but with no way to take it home with me on my flight to San Diego. So, at the airport, I gave it to somebody I met in Arrivals. You can only imagine the look on the guy's face when I presented him with this $500 bottle of wine (and my business card) dressed as I was in jeans and a T-shirt. As I scurried to catch my flight, I looked back at him thinking he must have thought I was crazy. And at that moment, I was more than a little miffed that I'd had to give such a gem of a wine to a total stranger!

But about a week later, I got an e-mail from the guy who told me he'd celebrated his tenth wedding anniversary with his wife, sharing my "wonderful bottle of wine" with her and a number of other people! His words made me feel *so* good, and I realized that in giving him an unexpected gift, an unexpected gift of gratitude and appreciation had come back to me!

Speaking of gratitude and appreciation, let me close this book by saying, "Thank you!" to *you* for buying and reading this book. I hope you can put the advice and ideas it contains to good use in the business and home entertaining you do in the future.

As you do, please know this: *Power Entertaining* is the product not just of my own work, ideas, and professional experiences as a sommelier. It also reflects suggestions, ideas, and input from many of my fellow sommeliers and wine professionals, people from whom I've learned so much professionally over the course of my 30-year career and from whom I continue to learn every day.

So, my final words of thanks in this book go to my fellow wine professionals. You guys are my buddies and trusted colleagues. This book wouldn't have been possible without your generous contributions of spirit and talent to my efforts!

Appendix A

Major Grape Varieties on Restaurant Wine Lists

As a power entertainer, it's important to be knowledgeable about different kinds of wines so that you have options when selecting wines to showcase at power entertainment events. Here's a brief overview of the major grape varieties that appear on most restaurant wine lists.

Cabernet Sauvignon

Pronounced: "Cab-air-nay So-veen-yawn"

Tastes like: Black currants, green or black olives, mint, old mushrooms

Produced in: California, Washington State, Oregon, New York, Bordeaux, France, Italy, Australia, Spain, and Chile

Pinot Noir

Pronounced: "Pee-no Nwahr"

Tastes like: Cherries, strawberries, prunes, spice, barnyards

Produced in: California, Oregon, Washington State, France, Germany, Italy

Riesling

Pronounced: "Reece-ling"

Tastes like: Apricots, peaches, honeysuckle, geraniums, petroleum

Produced in: California, New York, France (Alsace), Germany

Chardonnay

Pronounced: "Shar-doe-nay"

Tastes like: Apples, lemon, pineapple, melon, vanilla, butterscotch, slightly burned toast

Produced in: California, Washington State, Oregon, Idaho, New York, France, Italy

Chenin Blanc

Pronounced: "Shen-non Blahn"

Tastes like: Apples, pineapple, guava, vanilla

Produced in: California, Texas, France (Vouvray), South Africa

Gamay

Pronounced: "Gam-may"

Tastes like: Raspberries, strawberries, violets

Produced in: California, Oregon, France (Beaujolais)

Gewürztraminer

Pronounced: "Ge-wortz-tram-me-nair"

Tastes like: Cloves, cinnamon, lychee nuts, geraniums

Produced in: California, Oregon, France (Alsace), Italy, Australia, Germany

Grenache

Pronounced: "Gren-ahsh"

Tastes like: Grape jam, violets, rose petals

Produced in: California, France (Rhône Valley), Spain, Australia

Merlot

Pronounced "Mer-low"

Tastes like: Blackberries, black olives, chocolate, plum—a softer wine than Cabernet Sauvignon

Produced in: California, Washington State, New York, France, Italy, Australia

Muscat

Pronounced "Mus-cat"

Tastes like: Peaches, apricots, nuts, raisins, citrus

Produced in: California, France (Alsace), Italy

Sauvignon Blanc

Pronounced: "So-veen-yawn Blahn"

Tastes like: Herbs, hay, citrus, grapefruit

Produced in: California, Oregon, Washington State, Texas, France (Loire Valley, Graves), New Zealand, Australia

Semillon

Pronounced: "Say-me-yown"

Tastes like: Honey, milk, cream, melon, fig

Produced in: California, Washington State, France (Bordeaux), Australia

Syrah

Pronounced: "See-rah"

Tastes like: Black pepper, violets, plum, berries, licorice

Produced in: California, France (Rhône Valley), Australia, (Shiraz), South Africa

Zinfandel

Pronounced: "Zin-fan-del"

Tastes like: Berries, raisins, plums, chocolate

Produced in: California

I encourage you to become intimate friends with all the wines on this list, especially those you may not know or have never tried. Expanding your own wine palate will enable you to do the same for others at power entertaining functions!

Appendix B

Categorizing Wines by Quality and Taste

People sometimes ask me, "Eddie, are there different classes of wine, and if so what kind and quality of wine should I serve people?" This is a great question to which I have a great answer! I generally distinguish three classes or levels of wine. Each category has its own place in the life of a wine enthusiast. Use these categories as a way to make wine selections either for business events or for home entertaining purposes.

- *Beverage wines:* These are common everyday "jug" wines that exist for the pleasure of everyday drinking (consumption). They are "simple" wines, and most of them possess neither vices nor virtues. For example, they're neither long on taste and complexity nor disappointing in bitterness and tartness. They are meant to accompany foods as a beverage (like water or soda do, too) and should never be served with assertive foods. They go down easily and go well with everyday meals that you might have at work or at home with the family. Generally these wines sell for less than $15 a bottle.

- *Better wines:* These wines are a step above beverage wines. Their outstanding feature is a certain "fruitiness," a concentration of flavors intense enough to give each wine its own personality. These wines should be consumed young; most of them will not improve with age. These are "varietal" wines (grape variety distinguishable). These generally start at about $20 to $25 a bottle.

- *Best wines:* These are wines of distinction, representing the epitome of what winemaking is all about. They require aging, and through the process, they acquire a certain personality and finesse that is hard to describe to those who have never tasted one. These wines appeal to the experienced wine drinker, to those who recognize value in subtle differences and are willing to pay for excellence. These start at about $50 and go up from there.

FIGURE B.1   The Three Bs

Appendix C

Don't Let the Restaurant *Happen* to You

Has this ever happened to you? You find yourself entertaining a dozen important clients while attending an industry convention in a major US city. You're lucky enough to get a reservation for the group at a great restaurant on a busy night. You think you're all set. But are you?

On getting to the restaurant you discover that your table is not quite ready, so you and your group are invited to have a drink at the bar. Your guests disperse until beckoned and a touch of anxiety takes hold in you, as you worry about the level of service you're going to get that evening.

Finally you're seated, but now there's a bevy of people swarming over you: a wine steward, servers, the maître d', all of whom repeat the evening's specials to you at a fast clip. Somebody thrusts a wine list into your hands as the identified host of the evening. You want to take time to study the list but the pressure's on. Your guests are hungry, and the waitstaff is eager to take drink orders to move your table service along.

Are you feeling comfortable?

Eating in a "fine restaurant" can be a frenzied and even stressful experience, especially when a big city restaurant is dealing with a huge crowd, a weekend night, and a major convention in town. Like the airlines, many restaurants overbook and consequently get overwhelmed when diners arrive and nobody has cancelled their reservations. The waitstaff all hope to get through the evening with minimal complaints and maximum tips. But what about you? Who's taking care of you?

Here are some things you can do to ensure yourself a pleasant and relatively stress-free evening when taking guests out for dinner:

👍 When you make your reservations, ask to speak directly with the manager or wine director/sommelier.

👍 Tell the manager or wine director/sommelier that you want to spend as much time with your clients as possible and wish to pre-arrange as much of the dinner and drink service as you can. Decide right then and there if you are dealing with somebody who "gets" what you're requesting and is willing to work with you to help you achieve your goals. If your gut says they are not the right person, find another individual—or another restaurant! Remember, your success in entertaining your guests that evening is going to depend on the help of that person.

👍 Give the manager or wine director/sommelier your budget.

👍 Ask that the evening begin with champagne, as a surprise to your guests.

👍 Tell the manager you want two wines paired with the first course. (This is both original and entertaining.) Here are some possibilities:

- *A New World/Old World comparison:* Pit a California Chardonnay against a French white burgundy and ask your guests to discuss the comparative "food friendliness" of each.

- *A horizontal tasting:* Compare two wineries featuring the same grape. You might pit a Napa Sonoma Chardonnay against a Santa Barbara Chardonnay and ask your guests to discuss the stylistic differences between the two.

- *A vertical tasting:* Compare two vintages from the same winery. Taste and compare a 1998 Cabernet and a 2004 Cabernet.

👍 Ask the restaurant manager about the restaurant's signature menu items and go with them. Ask them what wines on the restaurant's list show best with these food items.

👍 If there's time, have the restaurant e-mail you their suggested food and wine pairings. Look them over and make your decision.

👍 Ask if they have a small private dining room.

👍 Ask them if they can provide crystal glassware. These can be rented at a nominal cost if not. Fine glassware provides a powerful impact.

👍 Have them decant all red wines! This adds a touch of class and sets *you* apart from others who might entertain your clients.

👍 With parties of 10 or more, see if the restaurant can serve red wines from magnum (double-size) bottles. Most restaurants don't carry these, but by calling them in advance, they will have time to special order them for *your* party.

👍 Finally, make arrangements to pay the bill ahead of time. You don't want to have the bill arrive at the table, as it destroys the mood of the evening.

Careful planning can take a lot of stress out of business entertaining, so you can focus on both your guests and the moment. Don't let the restaurant "happen" to you. Plan ahead, impress your guests, and enjoy yourself!!

Appendix D

Sample Wine Tasting Sheet

Université de Bordeaux II
Institut d'Oenologie
351, cours de la Libération
TALENCE

FICHE DESCRIPTIVE DE DEGUSTATION

Nom du dégustateur _____

Identification du vin _____

ASPECT		
	Couleur(intensité, teinte) *Intensity? Globality of coloration? Evolution from red to orange (showing age)?*	
	Limpideté *Brilliance? Or... Haziness?*	
	Autres observations *Viscosity: slow legs? (higher alcohol) fast legs? (lower alcohol) (warm climate) (cool climate)*	

ODEUR	
	Netteté *Clean? Off odors?*
	Qualité *Breed? Character? Common? Varietal distinction? Typicity? Terroir?*
	Intensité *One dimensional (simple)? Multi-dimensional (complex)?*
	Description *Aroma (young)?..........BOUQUET (aged, evolved)?*

COUT	
	Defauts eventuels *Volatile Acidity (VA) ? Brettanomyces (Brett)? Ethery Alcohols? Sulfite levels (SO2)?*
	Description { Attaque *initial impression, first 2 seconds, announcement of wine in the mouth* Evolution *is there a continuation of the first impressions? (Acidity responsible)* Fin de bouche ? *Agreeable? Disagreeable? (Why?... Aggressive tannins? Astringency? Fruit dried out?*
	Equilibre et structure générale *overall balance? Does it finish as well as it starts?*
	Persistance aromatique *complex bouquet? Aftertaste persistent?*

JUGEMENT	
	Autres observations *what stands out....positively? ....negatively?*
	CONCLUSIONS *wine of distinction? wine to buy? ready to drink? needs more time? Flawed?...what specifically is responsible for this? (Vinification?) (Poor vintage conditions?)*
	NOTESUR *grade* *8/20....15/20...19/20???*

FIGURE D.1 Sample Wine Tasting Sheet

Note: This is the standard tasting form used by all students at the Université de Bordeaux. I've noted (in italics) the specific qualities and characteristics the taster is to look for at each stage in the tasting of a wine. Download this chart from www.eddieosterland.com.

Appendix E

Eddie's Wine Tasting Sheet

Université de Bordeaux II
Institut d'Oenologie
351, cours de la Libération
TALENCE

FICHE DESCRIPTIVE DE DEGUSTATION

Nom du dégustateur *OSTERLAND, Edmund A.*

Identification du vin *POMEROL 1970*

ASPECT	Couleur (intensite, teinte)	*very intense garnet (typical 1970), not evolved, correct for 3 year old wine*
	Limpidite	*clear, quite brilliant*
	Autres observations	*legs are medium which makes me suspect alcohol level between 12.8 and 13.5%*
ODEUR	Nettete	*slightly ethery...not completely disagreeable, but...NOT CLEAN!*
	Qualite	*typical Pomerol, ripe fruit (currant, black cherry, plum...dominance of Merlot), coconut, vanilla (Oak)*
	Intensité	*good intensity (rich in aromatic elements)*
	Description	*young wine rich in aroma but, I suspect a slight note of volatile acidity*
COUT	Defauts eventuels	
	Description { Attaque	*lots of volume, very mellow fruit-forward attack*
	Evolution	*It starts well but it finishes hard with acetic overtones*
	Fin de bouche	*It finished vinegary, slightly bitter with negative tannins and out of balance*
	Equilibre et structure generale	*UNHARMONIOUS! It doesn't finish like it starts, I suspect the amount of volatile acidity of over 0.9 g/liter (threshold limit)*
	Persistance aromatique	*compromises the finish in a negative way (nailpolish-VA)*
	Autres observations	*it leaves an aftertaste that is both hard and sharp*
JUGEMENT	CONCLUSIONS	*this is a wine that, unfortunately has more flaws than qualities. It is particularly marked by volatile acidity in the finish. Completely disagreeable, vinegary, sharp and it burns the palate!*
	NOTESUR *8/20*	*Fault: Vinification problems, oxygen ...causing ethyl acetate*

FIGURE E.1 Eddie's Wine Tasting Sheet

Note: Actual exam given to me for finals and how I judged one of the wines I tasted, a 1970 Pomerol. My specific comments about the wine are in *italics*. Download this chart from www.eddieosterland.com.

Appendix F

How to Judge a Wine

Wine Evaluation Form

APPEARANCE
Color Intensity 1 ⟶
Color Intensity 2 ⟶
LIGHT   MEDIUM   SATURATED
AROMA
Quality 1 ⟶
Quality 2 ⟶
NONDISTINCT   DISTINCT
ATTACK
Fruitiness/Sweetness 1 ⟶
Fruitiness/Sweetness 2 ⟶
LOW/DRY   MEDIUM   HIGH/SWEET
EVOLUTION
Liveliness/Acidity 1 ⟶
Liveliness/Acidity 2 ⟶
LOW   MEDIUM   HIGH
FINISH
Persistence 1 ⟶
Persistence 2 ⟶
SHORT   MEDIUM   LONG

NAME WINE 1   YEAR

PRODUCER WINE 1

NAME WINE 2   YEAR

PRODUCER WINE 2

Wine Evaluation Form

APPEARANCE
Color Intensity 1 ⟶
Color Intensity 2 ⟶
LIGHT   MEDIUM   SATURATED
AROMA
Quality 1 ⟶
Quality 2 ⟶
NONDISTINCT   DISTINCT
ATTACK
Fruitiness/Sweetness 1 ⟶
Fruitiness/Sweetness 2 ⟶
LOW/DRY   MEDIUM   HIGH/SWEET
EVOLUTION
Liveliness/Acidity 1 ⟶
Liveliness/Acidity 2 ⟶
LOW   MEDIUM   HIGH
FINISH
Persistence 1 ⟶
Persistence 2 ⟶
SHORT   MEDIUM   LONG

NAME WINE 1   YEAR

PRODUCER WINE 1

NAME WINE 2   YEAR

PRODUCER WINE 2

Wine Evaluation Form

APPEARANCE
Color Intensity 1 ⟶
Color Intensity 2 ⟶
LIGHT   MEDIUM   SATURATED
AROMA
Quality 1 ⟶
Quality 2 ⟶
NONDISTINCT   DISTINCT
ATTACK
Fruitiness/Sweetness 1 ⟶
Fruitiness/Sweetness 2 ⟶
LOW/DRY   MEDIUM   HIGH/SWEET
EVOLUTION
Liveliness/Acidity 1 ⟶
Liveliness/Acidity 2 ⟶
LOW   MEDIUM   HIGH
FINISH
Persistence 1 ⟶
Persistence 2 ⟶
SHORT   MEDIUM   LONG

NAME WINE 1   YEAR

PRODUCER WINE 1

NAME WINE 2   YEAR

PRODUCER WINE 2

Wine Evaluation Form

APPEARANCE
Color Intensity 1 ⟶
Color Intensity 2 ⟶
LIGHT   MEDIUM   SATURATED
AROMA
Quality 1 ⟶
Quality 2 ⟶
NONDISTINCT   DISTINCT
ATTACK
Fruitiness/Sweetness 1 ⟶
Fruitiness/Sweetness 2 ⟶
LOW/DRY   MEDIUM   HIGH/SWEET
EVOLUTION
Liveliness/Acidity 1 ⟶
Liveliness/Acidity 2 ⟶
LOW   MEDIUM   HIGH
FINISH
Persistence 1 ⟶
Persistence 2 ⟶
SHORT   MEDIUM   LONG

NAME WINE 1   YEAR

PRODUCER WINE 1

NAME WINE 2   YEAR

PRODUCER WINE 2

FIGURE F.1 How to Judge a Wine

Note: Download this chart from www.eddieosterland.com.

About the Author

Eddie Osterland is an internationally acclaimed expert in the culinary arena of food and wine. For more than 25 years, he has delivered workshops and given highly entertaining and informative dinner talks to corporate audiences on power entertaining with wine and food.

Eddie has the distinction of being America's very first Master Sommelier, a wine expert who holds the prestigious degree of Diplôme Universitaire d'Aptitude à la Degustation (DUAD) from the Université de Bordeaux in Bordeaux, France. Upon completing his studies there, he went on to pass the grueling Master Sommelier Diploma in London in 1973 on his very first attempt! From there he went on to become head sommelier at the Hôtel de la Poste in Beaune, Burgundy, France—an American running a French wine cellar!

Today, Eddie is in great demand as a speaker, presenter, and wine and food coach. Crisscrossing the country, he speaks to more than 30 organizations a year, including such global companies as Accenture, General Mills, Citigroup, IBM, Merrill Lynch, GE, Ford, UBS, Discover Card, Sprint, Procter & Gamble, Oracle, and American Express. In 2008 he was the only Master Sommelier invited to entertain corporate clients at the China Olympics.

Known for his dynamic presentation style, warmth, and approachability, Eddie sees it as his mission in life to entertain and educate people about the joys of entertaining successfully with good wine and food.

Eddie is the Business and Entertaining Coach for Vistage International, the world's leading chief executive officer (CEO) organization, with more than 14,000 members worldwide. In 2008 he received Vistage's "100 Club" achievement award as one of the organization's most requested speakers.

Eddie appears frequently on radio and television to talk about the principles of power entertaining and how anyone can use these tools to create "dynamic food and wine experiences" for clients, business associates, friends, and family. He has been featured as a wine expert by *Esquire* magazine and serves as the official wine columnist for *Jetset Magazine*.

For more information about Eddie, visit his website at www .eddieosterland.com.

About the Collaborator

Richard Koonce (collaborator) is an executive coach, communications consultant, and former broadcast journalist who spent five years as a commentator on Public Radio's popular business program, "Marketplace." The author or coauthor of five previous books, including *Growing Leaders*, he is passionate about writing, entertaining, and fine food and wine (Barbera d'Asti and French burgundy are particular favorites!). Learn more about Richard's work at www.richardkoonce.com.

Resources

Keith Ferrazi with Tahl Raz, *Never Eat Alone* (New York: Doubleday, 2005), 95.

Michael Gibson, *The Sommelier Prep Course* (Hoboken, NJ: Wiley, 2010).

Edmund Osterland, *Wine and the Bottom Line* (Washington, DC: National Restaurant Association, 1980).

Rajat Parr and Jordan Mackay, *Secrets of the Sommeliers* (Berkeley, CA: Ten Speed Press, 2010), 72.

Emile Peynaud, *The Taste of Wine: The Art and Science of Wine Appreciation*. 2nd ed. (New York: Wiley, 1996).

Photo of Henry J. van der Voort is courtesy of his nephew, Yves de Boisredon, the Baron of Wine.

Index

Be outrageous . . . it's the only place where it's not crowded!

Starting from left to right: Steve Nemeth, Coleen Nemeth, John O'Neill, Mark Le Blanc, Art Feierman, Teresa O'Neill, Cathleen Haggerty, Colin Haggerty, and me on the stairs.